MW01611793

MORE
THAN A
GAME

HOW I FOUND THAT LIFE IS MUCH
MORE THAN FOOTBALL

———————

RICK GAGE

———————

FOREWORD BY MARK RICHT

Published in the United States by GO TELL
Ministries, Inc.
Initial manuscript by Marty Anderson
Edited by Dr. Don C. Berry and Pam Campbell
Cover design and layout by Seed™ Studios at
seedstudios.com
Previously published as *The Coach*,
ISBN: 0-9646473-1-1

The publisher expresses his appreciation to the people who allowed their stories to be included in this book. Because some of their stories are painful, the editors have, in some cases, changed the names and minor details to protect the identities of those involved.

Dedication...

To all the prayer partners and supporters of this ministry who help us in taking the life-changing message of Christ to the world.

Table of Contents

Acknowledgements

My sincere thanks...

To my Lord and Savior Jesus Christ for His grace, patience, and His desire that I should not perish but that I should come to Him in repentance.

To my lovely wife Lynne and precious daughters Sara and Anna. Thank you for understanding and supporting my call to be an evangelist. You are the greatest wife and daughters in the world.

To my mother Barbara and father Freddie who always pointed me to Jesus and encouraged me to follow Him.

To my three brothers—Daniel, Paul, and Rodney—all who are in the ministry. They are my closest friends.

And to Dr. Don C. Berry for encouraging and helping me to complete this book. He reached into my heart and helped put what was there on the printed page. I am thankful for his tireless work in providing rough drafts, rewrites, edits, and overall guidance in molding the message of this book.

Foreword

Rick Gage is a man I have admired for several years. In many ways, our lives have paralleled one another in college sports, in coaching, and in our commitment to the Lord Jesus Christ. I am honored to recommend his book, More Than a Game, to you.

As this book's title plainly says—and which I firmly believe, football is much more than a game. It is an arena where values are hammered out on the anvil of hopes, disappointments, discipline, and friendships. Rick and I both believe that Jesus Christ is the foundation for our values and the source of real life.

I teach our college players the principles of winning in life. Football is the lab where we practice what we've learned and sharpen our perceptions of what's important. I want these core values to sink deep into the hearts of our athletes, so they will live by them for the rest of their lives.

I believe in Rick, and I have had the privilege of being involved in his wonderful ministry. He is fulfilling God's calling in his life, and that's the best thing that can be said about any of us.

As you read this book, listen to God's Spirit as He inspires your heart with the message of the Gospel. Whether this is the first time or the 10,000th time you've been touched by Christ's forgiveness, respond with humility, thankfulness, and passion to please Him. This book is not about football; and actually, it's not about Rick Gage. It's about the wonderful grace of God who extends His love to you and me through Jesus Christ.

Mark Richt
Head Football Coach, University of Miami

CHAPTER 1

A ONCE-IN-A-LIFETIME OPPORTUNITY

I felt out of place in the elaborately decorated lobby of the Biltmore Hotel in Los Angeles. Yet as I listened to the robust, athletic young men around me, I felt the rush of excitement of being a part of the 1983 convention of the American Football Coaches Association.

We gathered in L.A. to attend clinics and seminars that would help us become the best coaches we could be. It was a time to experience the "perks" of mixing, mingling, and learning from the best minds in the game. It also was a time to celebrate victories . . . and forget defeats.

"Coach Rick Gage"—I liked the way it sounded. It made me feel like an equal among coaches I had always admired.

The coaching profession allowed me to stay fully involved with my first love—football. Even during the years I played college football, I had been driven by the burning desire to become a successful, admired major college football coach. I had been an assistant coach at Texas Tech University, a college located on the flat, dry plains of the Texas panhandle. For years, Texas Tech had been a member of the revered Southwest Conference, which included Texas, Texas A&M, TCU, Baylor, Rice, SMU, and Arkansas. My coaching career was beginning to take shape.

As I stood in the lobby of the Biltmore, I gazed through the glass doors to see if I knew any of the coaches who were arriving. Suddenly, I couldn't believe my eyes. There he was—the coach who had no equal, a living legend, one of the greatest college coaches of all time, and a sports hero of countless players and young coaches like me. Paul "Bear" Bryant was just stepping out of a limousine and walking into the hotel. Impulsively, I ran toward the door. After all, I thought, I might never have another opportunity to meet this larger-than-life coach.

"Coach Bryant, my name is Rick Gage," I blurted out as he opened the door. "I want you to know what an inspiration you've been to me. I hope some day I can accomplish as much as you have. Even half as much would make me happy."

Frankly, I don't remember much else. I was too awestruck to remember anything clearly except that I was actually talking with "Bear" Bryant, the coach who made Alabama football one of the greatest major college programs in America.

After he walked away, I realized what a dumb thing I'd said to him. How naïve could I be? Could anyone really expect to beat Coach Bryant's record? He spent 38 years in coaching, 25 of them at one school—Alabama. His teams chalked up 6 national championships and 15 victories in 29 bowl appearances. His won-loss record was an amazing 323 wins with only 85 losses and 17 ties. Of the athletes fortunate enough to play for him, 54 became

All-Americans and 47 became head football coaches. What a record! What a coach!

Only a few weeks later, on January 26, 1983, "Bear" Bryant unexpectedly died; but his legacy lives on. To this day, I can still remember Coach Bryant with his checkered houndstooth hat on his head, a rolled-up play script in his hands, leaning against the goalpost during pregame warm-ups, strolling up and down the sidelines, and later appearing before the press with his hoarse voice and kind face. That day at the Biltmore, I had taken advantage of a once-in-a-lifetime opportunity to meet my hero and the coaching idol of millions of football fans, young and old. "Bear" Bryant was one of college football's greatest coaches.

At the time, those brief words with "Bear" Bryant seemed like the most important few minutes of my life. But there was Someone else—Someone larger-than-life who had actively sought a personal, one-on-one encounter with me. For years, He had pursued me. He gave me a loving family and allowed me to hear the truth, but I had turned my back and gone my own way. He had tried to get my attention by showing me my desperate need for help, but I had closed my eyes to those needs. I lived for football because I thought it could fill the hole in my heart and give me the fulfillment I longed to experience. I can look back now and see that every major decision in my life was an opportunity to respond to the One who pursued me . . . or to go down my own path alone. Even from early childhood, I had been recruited for a different once-in-a-lifetime opportunity—the chance to know and serve the greatest Coach of all! Soon I would find out that life was much more than a game.

CHAPTER 2

BORN TO BE AN ATHLETE

The Gage family was already heavy on males when I came along in 1958—my dad Freddie, Daniel (six years old), and Paul (four years old). Since Daniel and Paul were already an inseparable duo, I grew up closer to friends than to my brothers. Seven years after me, Rodney, the last of the Gage boys, entered the fold.

Dad encouraged each of us to get involved in athletics. "Participation in sports," he declared, "is a good way to keep you boys busy and out of trouble." Keeping us out of trouble was of particular interest to Dad since he was away from home a lot. His advice was easy for me to follow. I didn't need any encouragement to get into sports because I was born to be an athlete. From my earliest years, I was described as "active," "tenacious," "strong-willed," "driven," even "stubborn." Those traits might cause problems around the house and in the classroom, but they are strengths for an athlete.

Daniel, my oldest brother, remembers family meals at restaurants. He related, "Rick was an innocent-looking toddler, but somehow it just came naturally for him to act up—especially when our family went out to eat. Nothing would stop him. Even our father's discipline in the restaurant restrooms didn't seem to phase Rick."

I was adventuresome with a mind of my own. Mom recalls that when I was three years old, I sometimes disappeared from the house and toddled across the street to the neighbors' house just to see what was going on. Meanwhile, she and the rest of the Gage family had no idea where I'd gone.

As she continued to deal with my bursts of energy, Mom attempted to confine me by having the yard fenced. She vowed to keep me corralled. She chose a lattice-type fence because she felt it would be more attractive than a chain-link fence. The fence builders came, completed the job, and started walking down the street toward their truck. Mom waved goodbye to them and stood back to admire her new fence. What she saw frustrated and confused her. In those few minutes, I was climbing over the top. Her "active, tenacious, strong-willed" three-year-old had already discovered how to turn an obstacle into an opportunity.

You can imagine how my hyperactive temperament affected my school experiences. I wish I had a dime for every time my exasperated teachers told me: "Sit still"; "Listen without talking"; "Be quiet"; "Leave him alone"; "Turn around"; "Get back in line"; and "Focus on the lesson." These were impossible commands for an energetic, unpredictable boy in perpetual motion. My teachers, it seemed, weren't too impressed with my energy and potential. When my family moved to the Houston suburb of Friendswood, the school required me to repeat the second grade.

In contrast to school, athletics were a breeze for me. It was no surprise when I became involved in organized sports at an early age. Dad used to say, "Rick, if they ever have to cut your head open, I know what they'll find—a ball of some kind."

As far back as I can remember, I was constantly either playing or thinking about sports—baseball, basketball, football. I had a ball of some sort in my hand every season of the year.

Frankly, I excelled in most everything that required physical action and skill. Even in elementary school, I started playing Little League football and, at the same time, riding and showing horses.

One year during the Houston Livestock Show and Rodeo at the Houston Astrodome, I won a third-place trophy riding my registered paint horse Sugar. As a tag-along teenager, I accompanied my brother Daniel and his friends to ride bulls at rural rodeos.

In addition to football and horseback riding, I was fascinated with boxing. Dad often told us boys about his street fights. Street-boxing (to be more accurate, "fist fighting") was the only sport Dad had been able to try firsthand while growing up in a very rough area of north Houston. I decided to try the sport. The hand-eye coordination I used in other sports translated easily to boxing, and I won a lot of matches. Today, Dad still speaks proudly of the amateur boxing matches I won during my junior high years.

But football was always my first love. Other sports and social activities were like sideshows to the main event. Football consumed my life from age nine to twenty-seven. This Don Quixote dream began with fourth-grade Little League and lasted until the day I resigned from Liberty University as an assistant coach. I loved every aspect of the game: the game plan and the execution, the individual accomplishments and the teamwork, the championship games and even the practices. As I advanced through high school and into college, I began thinking about making a career in the game I loved. I was born to be an athlete; but even more, I believed I was born to play and coach football.

CHAPTER 3

ACTING THE PART

Athletics was my first love, but another activity consumed much of my time and influenced my early years. As an evangelist, Dad preached in churches all across America. Naturally, my parents made sure that my brothers and I spent many hours each week attending Sunday school, morning and evening worship, and mid-week prayer services. In addition, we were expected to participate in many other church-centered activities. My mother even remembers dragging me along to the women's church groups when I was a preschooler. You've heard of families who were "in church every time the doors were opened." We were one of those families.

The whole Gage clan attended a multitude of evangelistic crusades where Dad spoke as well as those led by other well-known preachers. Throughout the years I was growing up, visiting pastors, evangelists, and missionaries were regular guests in our home, eating a meal or two or staying for a few days. In fact, the Gage house often seemed like a headquarters for ministers. As these visitors, other parents, and friends watched our family up close, some of them thought our parents were too strict in forcing us to attend church meetings so often. Today Dad readily admits his approach was a bit too demanding.

I remember being invited by a junior high teammate's family to a water-skiing weekend on Lake Austin. Dad said I could go on one condition: My friend's family had to agree to take me to church in Austin on Sunday morning. To say the least, I was terribly embarrassed to have to tell my friend and his parents about Dad's condition. As it turned out, while skiing early Sunday morning, my friend broke his wrist by crashing into the dock. "Church time" was spent at the nearest hospital, but I didn't mind that at all!

As one of the "Gage boys," I really had no choice about what services I would attend or in which programs I would participate. We attended every service and every event. I took some comfort and enjoyment, though, in the fact that I could hang out with some of my friends at youth meetings.

It took me a long time to understand why Dad was unwavering and insistent regarding church attendance. He had traveled to hundreds of churches across America to preach in evangelistic crusades and saw a lot of preachers' kids who never went to church. He still is distressed when he thinks of the prison crusades where he found some preachers' children serving time. A few were hard-core drug addicts arrested for armed robbery. Once he accompanied a preacher's son to a house of prostitution in order to rescue a wayward sister. Dad decided that his four sons weren't going to end up like many other PKs (preachers' kids)!

But Dad wasn't just concerned about his sons. He cared about all young people in trouble—particularly those from the poor and dangerous areas of Houston and other large cities across

America. Out of his commitment to reach young people, Dad started a boys' home in 1964. Teen Liberators later became known as Pulpit in the Shadows.

This ministry was nationally recognized as one of the first of its kind to effectively reach out to prodigal boys. Pulpit in the Shadows opened its arms to young drug addicts, many who had been mainlining—injecting heroin directly into their veins. Some of these young men were street criminals, stealing to sustain their $200- to $600-a-day dope habits.

The focus of the ministry was to help lost young people find a relationship with Jesus Christ and support them through the torturous cold-turkey of drug withdrawal and breaking free from the bondage they experienced as prodigals in the "far country." Lay people and ministers became rescue partners. Frequently, nationally known speakers spoke at the chapel services. I have vivid memories of those dramatic worship experiences of praise, preaching, testimonies, and prayers.

The word and the witness of what God was doing through Pulpit in the Shadows got out quickly. Youth on the streets of Houston, the police, government officials, and the religious community all heard about the miracles of changed lives. Pulpit in the Shadows was a place where God's love overflowed. Hopeless, helpless young people were saved by the power of Christ and given a new reason to live.

Growing up in the Gage household meant that I came under the influence of the Gospel of Christ and the witness of Christian ministry over and over again. Unfortunately, the Gospel message became a mere repetition of words to me. My soul became hardened, and the power of the Gospel didn't make a dent in my heart. Instead, the words of forgiveness and salvation were like water running off a duck's back.

I knew Dad's workplace was the church; therefore, I assumed the reason we attended church so often was because it gave us the opportunity to be near him. Church-going became a routine way of life. Although physically present at church, I was mentally in a very different place. I daydreamed of playing ball and having a good time with my friends. As I grew older, I learned how to act the part of being a "nice Christian boy." I played the role of a young Christian gentleman and knew how to impress church people. My Dad says I "could do a good snow job on most people." I didn't really understand what it meant to have a relationship with Christ; but I walked down the aisle of the First Baptist Church in Friendswood, Texas to make a profession of faith at the age of eight. I was presented to the church, shook hands with members of the congregation after the service, and returned that evening to be baptized. A few years later, I was the "All-American" teenager who could excel in athletics and be a fine, young Christian. The first part was true, but the second part was just an act.

CHAPTER 4

THE PRODIGAL YEARS

During my junior high years, I got tired of acting like a nice Christian boy. Gradually, I began more deliberately to rebel against my parents and my Christian upbringing. Jerry, a close friend since second grade, was always ready and willing to step outside the ethical boundaries that most of our friends grew up to respect. Besides being the biggest, toughest, and fastest guy in our class, Jerry was always mischievous. He was also a bully.

Every time Jerry "tested the waters" of independence and stepped out on a limb to take chances, I was right behind him. I was easily influenced—controlled may describe it more accurately—by Jerry's personality. He angrily and forcibly turned against anyone, even a friend, who got in his way. Sometimes peer pressure among young people isn't just a desire to please others; it's a desire just to stay in one piece!

Jerry and I belonged to "The Jocks," a group of athletes who hung out together on and off the athletic field. On weekends, we frequently attended parties, movies, and other events that our friends enjoyed. Several of us liked to camp out. We especially enjoyed staying out at a friend's farm because we could easily get booze and drink there. At my friend's farm, with the security and peer support of the rest of the group, I was introduced to alcohol, cigarettes, cigars, and other crazy stuff.

After completing driver's education classes, I proudly earned a driver's license on my sixteenth birthday, my freshman year in high school. Previously, I had only used alcohol and smoked with friends at parties; but now with a car, it would be much easier for me to go places and do things on my own. I could go anywhere I wanted to go, and I could make any choices I wanted to make. Still, I was careful to wear my Christian mask and protect the Gage reputation. I remained a faithful member of the Fellowship of Christian Athletes in high school. Our freshman football coach, who was a fine Christian, led us in team prayers, held Bible studies in his home, and talked about the Lord in and out of class. I was his loyal supporter.

Incidentally, during my freshman year, Friendswood High School won the Class AA Texas State Championship against Hooks High School which was ranked number one in the state. You may have heard of a great football player who came out of Hooks, Texas—Billy Sims, an All-American running back, Heisman Trophy winner for the University of Oklahoma, and two-time All-Pro for the Detroit Lions.

During my ninth- and tenth-grade years, I began running around with a close friend from a high school across town who introduced me to lots of his friends. Chuck's family and mine became devoted friends and remained so for years. We all attended the First Baptist Church of Pasadena, Texas where Dr. Darrell Robinson was pastor. Chuck and I spent many weekends together. We often went to the Pizza Inn on the

Square in downtown Houston where there was a live band and lots of beer! Although you had to be eighteen to be served beer, we usually found a crowd of young people who had enough beer to pass around.

During the summers of my high school years in Friendswood, I spent many evenings cruising Main Street with friends or hanging out in shopping center parking lots. Older guys almost always had abundant booze to pass around. Not only did this help pass the time, but it marked my passage from a dependent youth to a self-determined teenager.

I played junior varsity football during my sophomore year which spurred my interest in choosing to become a counselor at a summer sports camp. Chuck's dad, a former professional baseball player for the Boston Red Sox, was one of the camp's owners. Young people attended the camp from schools all across the country. The counselors consisted of athletes and students from various colleges and universities.

That particular summer, a camp counselor who played baseball for the University of Texas introduced me to marijuana. The first time I smoked a joint, I became dizzy and sleepy—and resolved I would never try it again! Later that summer, I started dipping tobacco, smoking cigarettes, and drinking beer regularly—and excessively.

Our varsity head football coach was very strict and wouldn't allow tobacco, drugs, or alcohol of any sort. Players caught were required to run a hundred miles (usually five miles a day for four weeks) before they could get back on the team. Several kids who were caught violating the rules quit the team rather than endure the ordeal of sitting out four weeks and running a hundred miles. Somehow, I managed to escape his notice and avoid this punishment.

Unfortunately, Sunday mornings came every week! To save face and keep my "Christian" image intact, I had to make an effort to be in Sunday school and church. The adult leader of our high school Sunday school department asked Chuck and me to lead the opening assembly before we broke into smaller groups. Pretending to be model "Christians" on Sunday mornings was often very difficult since we were very involved in the weekend party scene.

After Jerry's mother died and his dad remarried, my friend gained a new stepsister, Connie. She was a senior; Jerry and I were juniors. I took her to her senior prom at Houston's classy Warwick Hotel. Afterward, everyone went out to eat and then headed to Galveston where one of Connie's friends had a beach house. We "partied" all night and spent the next day at the beach, reenacting the rituals of other high school proms. After that weekend, Connie and I became "steadies" for several years.

During the summer between my junior and senior years, I worked in construction to help me prepare physically for my final year of high school football. It was imperative that I have a great year if I expected to have any real chance of playing college football. My primary goals in life were to play college football and later make a career of coaching. I had a great senior year, winning All-District as a defensive back and playing wide receiver.

Nevertheless, a successful senior year doesn't guarantee a full college scholarship. I got little attention from recruiters, so my high school coach sent letters of recommendation to colleges and universities across the country. I even visited colleges, showing them films of my better games. Several football programs invited me to try out as a walk-on, but none offered me the full scholarship I hoped to get. I was convinced a scholarship was the only motivation that would keep me committed to work hard to earn a college degree.

By the time spring arrived, Connie and I had temporarily broken up. Since I didn't have a date to the senior prom, a couple of friends and I decided to do our own thing. We bought some booze, drove down to Galveston, and cruised around town.

When I arrived home late that night, the house was dark and the front door was locked. I tried to crawl through the kitchen window and sneak into my room, but Mom was standing there watching me. She threatened to call Dad (who was away at a crusade) and tell him I was drunk. I knew if she did, when he got home, I would be history! She knew it, too. Maybe that's why she never told Dad. She disciplined me harshly and let me know—in no uncertain terms—that she was tremendously angry and disappointed in me.

Only a short time later, our family visited the Bay Area Baptist Church to hear Dr. J. Harold Smith, a world-renowned evangelist who was preaching a one-day crusade. That Sunday morning Dr. Smith preached his famous sermon, "God's Three Deadlines." I listened. His words became hammer blows to my heart. As I sat there, I asked myself: Rick, where are you headed? Here you are, a senior, preparing for a football scholarship, graduating from high school, considering your future. What is happening to your life?

I forced myself to take a good, hard look at the party scenes I had been involved in. I had been living carelessly with no concern for the consequences of my actions. How many times had I turned away from the convicting power of the Holy Spirit? How many pastors, evangelists, and Sunday school teachers had shared with me the Good News about Jesus Christ?

I began listening with my head and my heart. Dr. Smith told story after story, illustrating the lives of those who had turned away from God's Spirit and rejected Christ. Like me, they had heard the message of the Gospel. They too had a chance to be saved, but they didn't choose to follow Christ. Lost and disbelieving, they wandered away from God—or ran from Him. Their deadline had come and gone.

Dr. Smith's message pierced my heart like an arrow. Over and over, he detailed the dramatic accounts of people who had walked away without Christ. Then suddenly, these same people faced disastrous consequences of unforeseen financial ruin, the loss of a cherished family member, or an untimely, tragic death. They had crossed the line, God's deadline. They said an emphatic "no!" to God. Now judgment had come. For them, life was over and they faced an eternity without Christ.

Even though I had spent nineteen years in a Christian home, Dr. Smith's message of these tragic stories shook my complacency. What if I were to die today? I wondered. Have I committed the unpardonable sin? Is it too late for me? Where will I spend eternity?

When the invitation was given that Sunday morning to publicly make a commitment to Christ, a great number of people responded by going forward to the altar. I sat near the back of the church next to Mom, fighting the conviction that had struck deep in my heart. I gripped the back of the pew. I was torn up inside. I felt as if a raging battle was being waged for my soul. The questions pierced my soul: What am I going to do? Is this worship service my deadline?

Finally, I let go of the back of the pew and slipped into the aisle. I went forward—broken and emotionally crushed. I went straight to my Dad who was standing at the front, assigning counselors to those making decisions. I threw my arms around him, weeping on his shoulder, sobbing out the words: "Dad, I need to get right with God." We embraced each other for a long time. Dad was so happy; I knew his heart was about to burst. He immediately took me to the counseling room where he placed me with a counselor. The counselor took for granted that I knew all I needed to know about committing my life to Christ. After all, I was Freddie Gage's son. He said, "Rick, I'm sure I don't need to explain to you what it means to be saved." He was wrong.

Instead of explaining the Gospel to me and confirming a decision to trust Christ for salvation, the counselor brought me back to the auditorium. Dad had already shared with Dr. Smith that his son had trusted Christ that morning. The next thing I knew, Dad had me on the platform telling the congregation what God had just done in my life. I certainly wasn't prepared to speak publicly about my "changed life." I had to think about what to say, and I had to think fast! I shared briefly and simply that I had "just recommitted my life to Christ." Tears filled my eyes. I was very emotional and very broken.

Under deep conviction as a result of Dr. Smith's message, I had "rededicated" my life but what I needed was to be saved. You can't rededicate what has never been dedicated to the Lord in the first place.

What a morning! I had wanted desperately to experience God's grace and forgiveness, but all I felt was confusion and guilt. I know the counselor thought he was doing the right thing in assuming Freddie Gage's son understood the Gospel, but his assumption meant that I missed a golden opportunity to grasp the truth—and for that truth to grasp me. For the next months and years, I remembered the message of "God's Three Deadlines." Years later, God used the memory of Dr. Smith's words to lead me to a genuine salvation experience.

The next day I went back to school and ran into several classmates who had attended that powerful service. In response to my decision to "rededicate my life," I told myself that I was never going to drink again or conduct myself in such an offensive manner with my friends. I was surprised that I no longer had the same desire to be associated with my good drinking buddies; but on the other hand, I didn't want to be a "goody-two-shoes" either.

I was making choices to clean up my life, but I didn't have the inner strength God gives to His children. My long-time friend Jerry ridiculed my choices to try to live a better life, and he began calling me "Jesus." I felt humiliated. In spite of his condemnation, I began to pray and read my Bible consistently. I prayed about my future, about college, and that I would be granted a football scholarship somewhere. I was at the end of my senior year of high school. What did the future hold for me? Would I get a scholarship to play football after all? I trusted God for an answer. Then a letter arrived from

Blinn Junior College in Brenham, Texas.

Blinn invited me to their preseason football tryouts. As a member of the Texas Junior College Football Conference, Blinn's football team allowed only thirty-three players—all who were on full scholarships. If I made the team as a walk-on, they guaranteed me a full scholarship.

When Dad and I visited Blinn, we met Ben Boehnke, the head football coach who took us on a tour of the campus and helped us check out their academic requirements. I decided to enroll and report for football tryouts in August.

In preparation for those tryouts, I found a summer construction job. After each hard day's work, I went through a strenuous workout at the high school. Each evening I jogged, ran wind sprints at the stadium, and lifted weights at the field house. Our high school quarterback, who had received a scholarship at Kansas State, worked out with me, throwing passes so I could work on my receiving skills. Those summer days were painfully long, but I was absolutely determined to make the team at Blinn College. When August rolled around, I was ready both physically and mentally.

When I arrived at Blinn's football camp, I became immediately apprehensive: Seventy-five walk-ons had reported for tryouts in addition to those who were returning for their sophomore year. Only seven scholarships were available!

The coaches put us through various tests and drills to evaluate our athletic ability the very first day. I passed the mile run with the fastest time in camp. This gave me hope that I might make the team. Monday morning we dressed in full pads, and we started three strenuous two-and-a-half-hour practices a day. It didn't take long for some of the walk-ons to become walk-outs! And a few others who considered the practices entirely too strenuous quit before the official cuts began. Finally, through the process of elimination, one other player and I competed for the last available scholarship.

It came down to the final cut. Coach Boehnke told each of us he was having a hard time making a choice and that we should come back to his office that afternoon for his final decision. It was a tense, anxious time for both of us.

The moment arrived. All the players gathered in the locker room—dressed in their uniforms for team pictures. Coach Boehnke walked out of his office and came straight toward me.

"Gage, go get your uniform." I had made the team. Barely.

CHAPTER 5

COLLEGE FOOTBALL

Hooray! I was in college on a full football scholarship. My roommate Greg and I had been "matched up" at the August training camp. Little did I realize how close we would become and how much Greg's life would affect mine.

In some of our first conversations, Greg told me his dream of playing pro football, following in the footsteps of his cousin who played for the Buffalo Bills. After watching him perform as our starting linebacker, I realized that Greg was more than capable of reaching his goal.

I also was playing well at my position. In the first football game of my freshman year, I started at wide receiver. That year Blinn College played against Tyler, Wharton, Henderson County, Navarro, and Kilgore Junior Colleges. We played each team twice—once at home and once on their turf.

At the end of the season, four-year schools recruited several sophomores. Some stayed in Texas at well-known universities such as Texas, Baylor, Houston, and West Texas State. Others went on to play their junior and senior years out-of-state.

A standout sophomore teammate, Kirk Collins, was one of my buddies. Since he didn't have a car, I loaned him mine for dates or just to get off campus. Kirk's athletic ability impressed me greatly. He was a quiet, self-assured, good-looking athlete admired by his peers. No one was surprised when Kirk left Blinn to play at Baylor University where he became an outstanding defensive back.

In 1980, the Los Angeles Rams drafted Kirk in the seventh round. During the 1983 season, Kirk started at right cornerback and was leading the NFL in interceptions until he injured his hamstring. While examining him, doctors discovered cancerous tumors. Within a matter of months, Kirk died, leaving behind a wife and young son.

Blinn's players were scouted each year by four-year colleges because the college had so many good athletes. My teammate Leroy King was highly sought by a number of major universities. He chose the University of Texas where he replaced the legend, Earl Campbell, who had been drafted by the Houston Oilers. My successful freshman year sparked interest among recruiters from my favorite school, Baylor University.

I also had a productive year in the classroom. What a surprise! Academics were never my strong suit, but being awarded a full football scholarship gave me the incentive to discipline myself to do much better in class than I (and certainly my parents!) previously thought possible.

Another surprise came when I achieved social success in Blinn's party scene. Starters on the football team enjoyed campuswide recognition, and we received invitations to many social gatherings on and off campus. Going to bars and clubs became routine experiences for many of us.

Drugs and alcohol became rituals in my life. Why? It wasn't a matter of needing to be "accepted." I was already accepted and, to some extent, admired. I simply wasn't strong enough to say: "No!" Drugs flourished on campus—even in the football dorm. A teammate who smoked marijuana in high school continued his habit in college. Occasionally, when I visited his room, a marijuana joint would be passed around. Along with the others, I took a hit.

During this period of my life, if someone had asked me: "Rick, are you a Christian?", I would have said, "Yes." But my actions spoke otherwise. An authentic Christian should be under a greater conviction of guilt than I felt at that time. I felt convicted about my bad behavior but only by the fear of being caught!

In the spring of my freshman year, I experienced another life-changing event. I was driving back from Houston to Brenham one Sunday night after hearing Dad preach when another car struck me. The broadside crash hit the passenger side of my Camaro. The other driver was legally drunk. He had run a stop sign, slamming into my car between the passenger door and the back panel. The police estimated his speed at 50 mph. A split second sooner and his car might have gone right through me. My car was totally demolished, but I escaped with hardly a scratch. Looking back later, I wondered, Was God trying to get my attention?

At the beginning of my sophomore year, I injured my knee while playing our first scrimmage against Southwest Texas State University. My knee became very swollen and sore. Over the next couple of weeks, I visited several doctors and discovered that I had a torn cartilage in the left knee which would require surgery.

Recruiters from various four-year schools began showing up at Blinn's games. Clearly, no recruiter would pursue me since my knee injury prevented me from playing that fall. Football programs didn't want to take a chance that my knee might not heal completely—despite the fact that I had followed a strict rehabilitation program. The chance of getting a scholarship to Baylor, the school I had set my heart on attending, was zero. It seemed as if my football career was over.

Little did I know that an assistant coach from Cameron University in Lawton, Oklahoma was asking Coach Boehnke for a list of players he would recommend for their football program. My name was on that list! Seven of us were invited to fly to Lawton one weekend for an initial recruiting visit. I was extremely excited. I had almost given up hope of playing football again, but now I had renewed hope. Although Cameron was a NAIA Division I program, it was known to play a good brand of football.

What a weekend! When we arrived Friday evening, we were taken to the football dorm where we met some players who would be our hosts for the weekend. Several of them had played for Blinn during my freshman year, so I felt at home right away. That helped because the next stop on our schedule was something completely new to me. We were guests for a toga party at a local club. They wrapped us in sheets to re-enact the ancient Roman clothing. We arrived to witness a sea of people in similar trappings, and the party turned out to be a really wild night.

Later that weekend, all of us who flew in

from Blinn met with the coaching staff and were offered full football scholarships. Not all accepted, but I sure did! After all, no other college was waiting on my doorstep. Three other Blinn teammates accepted scholarships along with me.

At the end of that fall semester at Blinn, I went home for the Christmas holidays before transferring to Cameron. The Cameron coaches were aware of my knee problem and knew it would probably take approximately six months to heal from surgery. After months of rehabilitation, by April when spring training started, my knee had fully healed. I was ready to play; and at the end of spring training, I won a starting position as a wide receiver. That next season I played exceptionally well—in spite of a losing record.

In the spring of my junior year, Connie and I broke off our relationship for good. She was working in Houston, and my move to Oklahoma made it a lot harder for us to see each other on a regular basis. After three years of dating, Connie was ready for marriage; but I didn't want to endanger my football career, my athletic scholarship, or graduation from college.

Weeks later, I met Joyce, a cheerleader at Cameron University. She had grown up in Lawton, Oklahoma; and her parents were active in the First Baptist Church. For the first time since leaving home, I began attending church—occasionally. Joyce and I continued dating for the next four years.

During my junior year, the Cameron coaches successfully recruited several quality players who transferred from schools such as Oklahoma, Kentucky, Texas, Texas A&M, and LSU. This helped produce a strong, winning team during my senior year that resulted in an invitation to play a small college bowl game—the Boot Hill Bowl in Dodge City, Kansas. We defeated Adams State from Colorado. I was sure this bowl victory and my Bachelor of Science degree in Health and Physical Education the following May would enhance my chances of landing a good coaching job after graduation.

My success at Cameron University was interrupted during my final year by tragic news: My old Blinn roommate, Greg, and his fiancée had been killed when a train hit their car. The news hit me like two blows from a sledgehammer. I had lost a good friend, and I had let him down. Here I was, Rick Gage, a preacher's kid, a professing Christian; but I never shared the Gospel with Greg. I never asked him if he was saved. I felt shocked when I heard about his death, but my deep grief was coupled with gnawing guilt.

As the end of my senior year drew near, I began to consider my options for the future. I wanted to stay as close to football as possible. I'll always remember my college days as some of the greatest years of my life. While I realized that my playing career was over, I still had dreams of becoming a successful coach.

CHAPTER 6

FULFILLING MY DREAM

In May of 1981, I graduated from Cameron University. That same spring I began to look for a coaching position at a high school or a college. In June I was offered a high school coaching job in the Houston area at Clear Lake High School.

I was faced with a dilemma: I really wanted to coach on the college level, but the opportunities seemed limited. The end of summer, along with football training camps, was rapidly approaching. Football staffs would soon be getting ready for players to report and begin the rigorous two-a-day practices. I decided to sign a contract to coach and teach at Clear Lake High School. Within a couple of weeks, I was attending the annual Texas High School All-

Star Football Game at Texas Stadium in Dallas.

At half-time, Coach Keith Lavendar, my college coach at Cameron, introduced me to Bill Young, the head coach at West Texas State University, who was looking for a graduate assistant to coach their tight ends and work with the offensive line. I told him of my interest and said that I'd be willing to fly up the following week to meet with him. I flew to Amarillo and spent a day and a half touring the university and getting a thorough briefing on their football program. All went well, and Coach Young offered me the position.

During that same time, I was also in contact with Coach Jerry Moore at Texas Tech University. He told me that Tech had a graduate assistant position open, but he had already offered it to another coach and was waiting for a response. I really wanted that coaching position because Texas Tech was a major university in a major conference. To my disappointment, the other coach accepted the job. I now had to decide whether to accept the position at West Texas State. But could I in good conscience cancel my contract with Clear Lake High School? I decided to talk to the Clear Lake head coach about my situation. After sharing my desire to coach at West Texas State, he released me from the contract.

I was now a college coach! Not much fame and fortune, to be sure; but I was taking another big step toward fulfilling my dream of becoming a prominent, successful coach. I moved to Canyon, Texas and became a part of Bill Young's coaching staff. West Texas State was a member of the Missouri Valley Conference which included Tulsa, Wichita State, Southern Illinois, Drake, New Mexico State, Indiana State, and Illinois State. Our non-conference games included Iowa State, University of Nevada–Las Vegas, and Louisiana Tech.

I was now in the big leagues, but I quickly learned that playing four years of college football didn't automatically prepare me for diagnosing and coaching the Xs and Os offensively and defensively. Being young, single, and willing, I was committed to work hard to become the best coach possible.

Coach Young was a committed Christian, and he believed people ought to learn life's spiritual lessons. He began each staff meeting with a devotional and prayer. I was impressed and blessed. These were familiar surroundings that helped reconnect me to the Christian influences under which I was raised. I quickly played the role and acted the part, participating in Christian activities and repeating what I had said so many times before. Periodically, I was asked to lead some of the staff devotions.

In spite of my shallow religious commitment, that first season helped mature me quite a bit and I became extremely excited about the opportunity to coach on the college level. I especially enjoyed flying to cities like Aimes, Iowa to play Iowa State and to Wichita, Kansas to play Wichita State. Then on to Las Cruces, New Mexico to play New Mexico State and to the bright lights of Las Vegas where we battled the University of Nevada–Las Vegas. As a young football coach, I thought I had arrived! I had put a lot of long hours into this first season of my coaching profession, and I had done a good job. Didn't I have a right to be proud?

My recruiting territory on behalf of the West Texas State football program was Fort Worth and the plains of North Texas. At the end of the season, I hit the recruiting trail, visiting high school coaches and looking for prospects. At the end of the fall semester, Coach Young accepted the head coaching job at the University of Texas–El Paso. I wondered, What's my future going to be here at West Texas? Will I still have a job? I had been there only five months. There were a couple of options to consider.

Coach Jimmy Johnson, former coach of the Dallas Cowboys, was then the head coach at Oklahoma State. He and Coach Young were friends, and Coach Young had recommended me to Coach Johnson who was looking for an assistant to help coach the offensive line. I arranged a meeting with Tony Wise, the head offensive line coach, to discuss the possibility of helping him at Oklahoma State. (Incidentally, Tony Wise went to the University of Miami with Jimmy Johnson where the Hurricanes won a National Championship. Later, he went to the Dallas Cowboys to become Coach Johnson's offensive line coach. The Cowboys won two Super Bowl championships. Coach Wise then became the offensive line coach of the Chicago Bears.)

Another contact brought me back to Coach Jerry Moore at Texas Tech. That spring of 1982, Coach Moore wanted to bring on an additional assistant coach, so I caught a plane to Lubbock and met with him. He agreed to hire me; so in a couple of weeks, I moved to Lubbock and began coaching at Texas Tech University. Coaching in the Southwest Conference at Tech was certainly a step up from West Texas State. I felt I had made it to the major leagues! I was an assistant coach at a major university, and I was only 24 years old! I was climbing the success ladder and reaching for the top.

My responsibilities included helping coach the wide receivers and coaching the Texas Tech Junior Varsity. My first fall, I traveled to other cities on weekends to scout our upcoming opponents and pick up their game films. Some of the opponents I had to scout included the University of Washington, the University of Arkansas, Texas A&M, TCU, and Air Force. These trips were exhilarating but tiring. I was exhilarated to visit parts of the country and universities I had never seen before, but I was exhausted by so much travel, so much time in bars, and so much time alone. Somehow, though, I felt proud and invincible as a representative of Texas Tech football.

During this period, my life began to slide downhill. I went with the other young coaches on the staff at Texas Tech for a few drinks after practice or following a Saturday game. And a few drinks often turned into a few too many. We frequently hooked up while on recruiting trips or while attending coaching conventions and alumni functions. I was caught up in a lot of the worldly activities that go on in the coaching profession. After all, this was the Southwest Conference! We were expected to work hard. Why then shouldn't we play hard? Little by little, slowly and steadily, I began to drift farther and farther away from the right kind of thinking and the right kind of living. Gambling, smoking, using marijuana and then cocaine became commonplace.

One Saturday morning during spring training, we had just finished an intra-squad scrimmage. At noon some Texas Tech alumni and supporters were putting on a big barbecue for the whole team. The alumni who were sponsoring the meal were big partygoers themselves. After the barbecue, several alumni and coaches gathered inside a motor home on the athletic dining hall parking lot. As we were drinking and talking, somebody got the wild idea of taking a trip to Las Vegas.

The next thing I knew, some of us had agreed to catch the next plane out of Lubbock that very evening. That's exactly what we did! A couple of Tech supporters said they would take care of all the expenses and give us extra money for gambling when we arrived in Las Vegas. We left Lubbock immediately and stayed at the Las Vegas Golden Nugget until Sunday about noon. It was a crazy, wild weekend—another evidence that my life was completely adrift, cut loose from stabilizing convictions and strong, moral decisions.

In the fall of 1982, Coach Moore assigned me to work with the running backs. For the next year and a half, I worked side by side with Coach Rodney Allison. Rodney had been an All-American quarterback at Texas Tech under Coach Steve Sloan. He was famous in Lubbock and respected by all the Texas Tech alumni.

Rodney and I became very close friends, and we remain close friends to this very day. Among the talented athletes we coached was a young player named Timmy Smith who later played for Coach Joe Gibbs of the Washington Redskins. (You may recall that Timmy had a big game in Super Bowl XXII where he rushed for more than 200 yards in the Redskins' win over the Denver Broncos.)

People in the coaching profession have an ever-present, ominous, dark cloud always hanging over their heads. If your team is losing, there's no job security. Year after year, coaches must win enough games to keep their jobs. During my two years at Texas Tech, we had a 1-9-1 and a 4-7 record. At the end of our 1983 season, Coach Moore's job was on the line so he made some changes in the coaching staff. I happened to be one of those changes. Coach Moore told me he would not be retaining me, but he would do everything he could to help me find another coaching position. I pursued other opportunities but began to realize that I had dug a deep pit for myself. My relationship with Joyce also had come to an end.

I was miserable. For years I had ignored God and made decisions to advance my career at all costs. I had made selfish choices, and I had turned my back on spiritual values. I had chosen the low road and had come to a dead-end in my life. I was down, discouraged, and very depressed. I was desperate to reach out and find someone to help me.

Rick, I tried to convince myself, get away. Go somewhere with your close friends. Then you'll feel better, and it'll take your mind off your problems. I called a friend in Houston. We planned a trip to New Orleans to see the Saints play the Houston Oilers.

I hoped some fun with a friend would get me out of my gloom and doom; but bright lights, bars, and a wild time in "Sin City" weren't the prescription that would heal my soul. Again, I took the wrong path. Satan had deceived me. He always offers immediate satisfaction of our lower, self-centered nature. He convinces us it is easy to find peace and happiness: "Just follow me, and I'll take care of the rest."

Looking back, I now wonder: Why didn't I turn to the Lord at that time? Why didn't I reach out to Christian friends or to my parents who loved the Lord and who loved me?

Do you remember the gospel story of the rich, young ruler who came running to Jesus? I too was running, but I wasn't running to Jesus. I was running away—away from Jesus and away from my problems. I tried to run away from emptiness, hurt, and loneliness; but like the Prodigal Son, I was in a far country—away, far away from the Father's house, and finding far more misery than ever before. It was foolish to think that a trip to Bourbon Street would fill a life that was empty, cover the hurts in my heart, or alleviate my desperate loneliness.

CHAPTER 7

TEMPORARY RELIEF OR A PERMANENT CURE?

Christmas 1983 should have been a festive, upbeat season of joy, but I was sad and lonely and frustrated. I spent the holidays with Mom, Dad, and the rest of the family. I knew my days at Texas Tech were numbered, so I decided to attend the national convention of the American Football Coaches Association in Dallas during the second week of January. It had been just a year since the Los Angeles convention when I met Coach Bryant. The week ended up being one of partying with other coaches and lobbying to find another job. I looked hard, but I found no opportunities. I went back to Mom and Dad's house for another night before leaving for Lubbock.

Dad told me that James Robison, a dynamic evangelist and longtime friend of the Gage family, would be preaching in a Lubbock church the following Sunday. As I prepared to leave, Dad encouraged me to go hear James preach.

On Sunday evening, I went to the Trinity Church to hear James Robison preach. He spoke about people being in bondage and needing to be set free. He told us how, in the Old Testament, the prophet Isaiah said the Son of God would come "to bind up the brokenhearted, to proclaim freedom for the captives and release from darkness for the prisoners" (Isaiah 61:1).

I knew I was a captive. I was in bondage because of self-centered choices, and I was a prisoner of my own desires. James Robison said God could set captives free from whatever was binding them. His message pierced my heart.

I needed to be set free—set free from a careless, prayerless, rebellious lifestyle. I was lonely, discouraged, and hurting inside. I was tired—tired of running away from God, tired of holding up my defenses, and tired of hearing my excuses. I didn't have any peace. I was hedged in—bound by guilt and broken by the conviction of personal sin, and I had no assurance of where I would spend eternity. All I could do was approach God in repentance and faith. When the invitation was given, I was finally ready to totally surrender my entire life to Christ. I went forward and knelt down on my knees at the altar and cried out to God for forgiveness.

Immediately, I felt as if a huge weight had been lifted from my heart. I was free from the bondage of sin that had dominated my life for so long. The Holy Spirit used the sermon that night to penetrate the hardness of my heart. God's love captured me and turned my life completely around. I still have a copy of the message James preached that night.

James knew every member of the Gage family, but he had no idea I was attending the service. When he saw me on my knees at the altar, he came over and asked me if I wanted to say anything to the congregation. "No," I said, "I just want to take care of business right here with God."

James told the congregation there was a young man at the altar. Then he said something I have never forgotten: "I would have flown all the way from Fort Worth to Lubbock just to see this young man give his life to Christ." That meant a great deal to me, but I was even more amazed that God had come all the way from heaven to earth to see me totally commit my life to Him. After the service in a back room, I privately shared with James what God had just done in my heart. He rejoiced and encouraged me to sell out and live completely for Jesus.

Seven years earlier, in 1977, while hearing Dr. J. Harold Smith preach on "God's Three Deadlines," I was a confused, scared young man seeking temporary relief from the consequences of my sin. I was overcome with what the Bible refers to as "worldly sorrow" (2 Corinthians 7:10), that is, a self-centered sorrow over the painful results of getting caught and feeling guilty. As I look back to that earlier conviction, I wonder if I wasn't stirred emotionally by the atmosphere of worship, praise, preaching, and testimony.

But on this night in 1984, I found Jesus Christ

as the permanent cure for my sin problem. Christ became the Savior of every fiber of my being. Previous worldly conviction had touched only my emotions. Now a godly sorrow led to a genuine repentance and conversion. Christ changed my emotions (feelings), my intellect (beliefs and thought patterns), and my will (desires and choices).

That night the Holy Spirit became a part of my life in a way I had never experienced before. I know the Holy Spirit used the godly influences of family and friends from years before to bring me to Christ. How thankful I was (and continue to be) for a Christian home, evangelistic preaching, church ministries, Christian friends, pastors, coaches, Bible study, and prayer. In the fullness of God's time, Rick Gage, the prodigal, returned home and was embraced by his Heavenly Father.

I was forgiven. My heart was clean. I was finally at peace with God and with myself. I left that night as a new man with a new heart and new life. I went straight home and called Mom and Dad to share what God had just done. It was 3:00 in the morning when I put down my

Bible. Peace at last. I went sound to sleep.

The next morning I walked into the Texas Tech football office to tell the coaches what had happened to me the previous evening. I shared with them that Jesus Christ had forgiven me and set me free. Coach Moore was there along with several other coaches, including our strength and conditioning coach, Mike Mock. Mike, a committed Christian, invited me to a Bible study. Each Wednesday at 3:00 a.m., a group of men met in a home to study Scripture and pray. I was there the following Wednesday morning. Two weeks later, I went to James Robison's Bible Conference in Dallas. From that point on, my life has been on track for Jesus.

Football had been my first priority for many years. Coaching was my life's dream, and winning was my goal. God had been on the sidelines of my life. I had put Him on the bench; but I learned that God won't stay on the bench, and He doesn't remain on the sidelines forever. He demands to be "The Head Coach" of my life—and yours.

As Coach, God confronts us in conscience and in circumstances. One day He will confront us in eternity. I had wanted to be an admired, successful coach; but my game plan excluded God. I had run my life my way. That way seemed good and right; but it was the path of destruction, emptiness, and frustration.

Shortly after my conversion experience, I officially resigned from coaching at Texas Tech. Dad encouraged me to accompany him on a revival crusade at Mount Pisgah Baptist Church in Austell, Georgia, just outside Atlanta. Dr. James Rock was the pastor. When we arrived Saturday evening, we checked into our hotel and went immediately to the church for a pre-crusade youth rally. The church was packed wall-to-wall with young people who had come from surrounding churches.

Steve Bartkowski, a two-time All-Pro quarterback for the Atlanta Falcons, was the special guest that night. Dad asked me to share my testimony before Steve spoke. It was the first time I had ever stood before an audience with a clear conscience and a clean heart. I told the group how Jesus had just changed my life.

God used that crusade to bring many souls to Christ. Each night, two hours before the crusade service, we met with the young people. We divided into small groups and went out to visit their lost friends. We tried to persuade them to come to the revival service each night, so they could hear God's Word and respond to the saving message of the Gospel.

One night after church, a lady handed me a piece of paper with the name and address of a family named Mote. She asked if I would go visit them. I had been saved only a few weeks, but already God was using me to bring others to Jesus Christ.

The next evening before the service, two of us went to visit Ronnie Mote and his family. It was a dreary, rainy night. We weren't sure of the directions, but God got us there without any difficulty. We drove down a long dirt road and came upon a rundown shack surrounded by trees. We knocked on the door, and a lady answered. Small children were standing beside her. When we asked for Ronnie, she told us he was cutting wood in the backyard. In a few moments, Ronnie came into the house. We told him and his wife we were from Mount Pisgah Baptist Church and that some friends had asked us to come and visit. I opened the Bible and shared the plan of salvation with the whole family. Before we left, the Holy Spirit used our witness and our tears to bring all of them to Jesus. The next night Ronnie and his family were in the crusade service.

Throughout the week, we visited young people, working in the "harvest fields" to reach as many of them for Christ as possible. Each day we went to area high schools to speak to Fellowship of Christian Athlete groups, football teams, and youth assemblies. God's Spirit moved mightily. In five nights, more than 450 people—many of them youth—recorded their professions of faith. Dr. Rock claimed this was "the greatest revival in the history of this church." Above all, it was the testimony of God's great work.

Dr. Rock asked me to prayerfully consider returning to become their youth director. Hundreds of new, young converts needed help to grow toward spiritual maturity. I prayed a lot. This was an important transition time in my life. Soon God's direction was confirmed, and I was certain the Lord wanted me to return and work with these young people.

I began my work by launching a dynamic youth ministry centered in Christ's call to salvation and spiritual growth. Every Sunday night, we taught the young people how to share their personal testimonies and the Good News. On Tuesday nights, we followed up with personal witnessing and visitation. In addition, I led a weekly Bible study on Wednesdays to help young people understand what it means to follow Jesus. God poured out His blessing, and many students in the community came to know Christ as their Lord and Savior.

In spite of the exciting youth ministry at Mount Pisgah, I missed coaching football. This desire was still in my heart. I called Dad and told him about my feelings. He encouraged me to travel with him in evangelism until I landed a coaching job.

While working with Dad, God used me in an unexpected and wonderful way. For the first time, I began to understand what my father had been doing during his last forty years of living and breathing the message of the Gospel. Leading lost souls to Jesus involved a lot of work and unflagging dedication.

A promising contact for a coaching job finally came in May 1984. Dal Shealy, the head football coach at the University of Richmond (Virginia), needed a replacement for his wide receiver coach who had become the head coach at Liberty University. Dal is a committed Christian coach who knew of my relationship to Christ. (Later, Dal became the president of the Fellowship of Christian Athletes.) Although he already had offered the position to someone else, he recommended me to Morgan Hout, the newly selected head coach at Liberty. The Lord used Dal's recommendation and my Dad's close ties to Liberty University and to its Chancellor, Dr. Jerry Falwell, to open this door of opportunity. I caught a flight to Lynchburg, Virginia; had my interview with Coach Hout; and was offered the running back coaching job—the same position I had held at Texas Tech.

I was excited! As quickly as possible, I moved from Dallas to Lynchburg. I look back on the doors God was opening, and I see that He was surrounding me with great men of God who strongly influenced me and became the Lord's instruments to call me into His ministry.

The years at Liberty were two of the greatest years of my life. Not only was I able to do what I loved to do—coach football, but also I was in a solid Christian atmosphere. For years, I had heard about the exciting ministries of Liberty University, Jerry Falwell, and "The Old Time Gospel Hour." Now I could enjoy the blessings of these ministries in "up close and personal" ways.

Many people connected with Liberty University and Thomas Road Baptist Church knew of Freddie Gage. Dad preached some very successful crusades at Thomas Road and Liberty over the years. These people who had been touched by my father's ministry warmly welcomed me.

The football program that we took over was in need of a major overhaul. Morgan Hout and his new coaching staff were committed to turning the program around. We worked long and hard. Our staff meetings began at 6:00 a.m. We worked sixteen- to eighteen-hour days during the football season, and the hard work paid off. Although our first season ended with a 5-6 record (better than the year before), there were many positive signs that we were well on the way to turning around a football program that had tremendous potential.

In the last game of 1984, we defeated the two-time NAIA National Champions, Carson-Newman, by a score of 27-14. We finished the 1984 season second in the NCAA II in passing, averaging 304.8 yards a game. The offense averaged 25.4 points a game and scored 30 or more points in five games. Our starting quarterback that season, Phil Basso, broke all passing records for Liberty, throwing for 3,226 yards and 24 touchdowns. He was first in the final NCAA II polls in yards passing, touchdown passes, and pass completions. He signed as a free agent with the Indianapolis Colts. One of our wide receivers, Freddie Banks, an Associated Press All-American, finished first in the final NCAA Division II receiving statistics, averaging 7.0 catches per game. His 77 receptions and 1,029 yards receiving were both Liberty single-season records. He became the first Liberty football player drafted by the NFL when the Cleveland Browns made him their fourth overall pick in 1985. Later, he was traded to the Miami Dolphins.

We took a program that was down and immediately injected life to it. Good things began to happen to the total football program because we made sure that we put Jesus first and football second. Each staff meeting started with devotions and prayer.

A spiritual highlight for the coaching staff was attending chapel services each Wednesday morning to hear Dr. Falwell speak. It was a great honor to sit under his preaching and leadership. He always expanded my vision and motivated my life.

Those brief years at Liberty University as an assistant football coach were days I'll always cherish. Slowly, day by day, with growing certainty, God was taking the desire to coach out of my heart. He replaced it with a greater desire to serve Jesus Christ in a full-time ministry.

As I sensed God's call into the ministry, I sought out various men and asked, "How can I know if God is really calling me to preach? How can I be sure He's calling me into the ministry?" I'll never forget the counsel and wisdom I received from Dr. Falwell, Sumner Wemp,

Manley Beasley, and others.

Brother Manley told me if God was truly calling me, I would be miserable doing anything else. He told me plainly, "Rick, you'll never be able to get away from that call." How right Brother Manley was.

When I left his home in Euless, Texas, I took a plane to New Orleans for the 1986 convention of the American Football Coaches Association. I found I had no desire to mix and mingle with coaches in the loose and immoral ways as I had done many years before. The seminars and social events didn't interest me anymore.

Brother Manley was right —I was miserable in that environment. I just wanted to be alone. At that moment, the Lord provided a very special witness. Each night during the convention, the Fellowship of Christian Athletes sponsored a Bible study and prayer time for coaches. I slipped into the meeting and praised God for the witness of those coaches who were committed to Christ.

The convention activities dragged on, and I was so restless that I decided to fly back to Lynchburg a few days early. Returning home, I stayed in my apartment the rest of that week, earnestly praying and seeking God concerning my decision to surrender to full-time ministry. I worried and began to second-guess the Lord. I questioned myself: What would I do, and what would my future be if I made this decision?

The devil was working on me relentlessly, assaulting me with every reason why I shouldn't follow God's calling. Nevertheless, in the midst of those doubts and questions, I clearly heard God quietly speaking to my heart: "Rick, I have already chosen you and called. Now I am waiting on you to take that next step of faith."

CHAPTER 8

CHANGING FIELDS

On the Monday morning after the American Football Coaches Association Convention and wrestling with my decision, I walked into Coach Hout's office and told him that God had been dealing with me for quite some time to direct me into the ministry full-time. I was still in the game, but I was changing fields.

I told Coach Hout, "Coach, I have to resign my coaching position and obey God's calling on my life." Instead of trying to talk me out of it, he was happy for me and affirmed the decision I had made. He said he was sad to lose me, but he would support me 100 percent. I remained on the coaching staff through the end of the recruiting season and then officially resigned.

Next I enrolled in Liberty Baptist Theological Seminary and began taking Bible courses. Simultaneously, I worked in the soul-winning ministry of the "Old Time Gospel Hour" with evangelist J. O. Grooms, a modern-day Apostle Paul. God continued to prepare me for His ministry through the influences of godly professors and ministry mentors. He also gave me cherished Christian friends and a new, strong desire to study the Bible.

I began to meet with some fellow seminary students on a weekly basis. We read a Christian book or studied the Word together in our homes. On Friday or Saturday nights, we often drove to a mountain outside Lynchburg, arriving around 12:30 or 1:00 a.m., where we would pray for hours—sometimes all night long. These prayer meetings revolutionized my prayer life. We challenged each other to live for God, holding each other spiritually accountable. Even today, I still stay in touch with these friends.

A few months later, I received an invitation to serve as an associate evangelist with Dr. Bailey Smith and Real Evangelism in Houston,

Texas. At the end of the seminary's spring semester, I moved to Houston to join the Real Evangelism crusade team. For five years, I traveled back and forth across the country as their youth evangelist, proclaiming the Gospel in evangelistic crusades and conducting school assemblies and youth rallies.

My special assignment was to reach the youth in all of our crusades. Therefore, I conducted and led pre-crusade youth rallies and soul-winning blitzes in towns all across the country. We saw many young people saved before the crusade ever officially began.

The goal was simple and focused. I was there to help young Christians become "soul" conscience and help them experience a personal burden for their lost friends. I trained young people how to share the plan of salvation and lead their friends to Jesus Christ. Then on Friday and Saturday nights, our evangelism team took them out on the streets, penetrating and saturating the hot spots of their communities with the Gospel. Hundreds came to know Christ personally because of these soul-winning blitzes.

One young lady who was actively involved in

one of our crusades wrote me a heart-warming letter:

Dear Rick,

I just wanted to thank you for the difference your ministry made in my life as well as for the impact it had on the youth of my community.

Through the truths you shared from God's Word, the examples you set, and the constant encouragement you gave, soul-winning has a new meaning in my life. I look at people around me as possible lost souls; and instead of waiting for opportunities to share the Gospel, I now look for opportunities to share.

One of the most meaningful events of the crusade was the impact your ministry had on the youth. Several evangelistic teams have been in our area, but I have never seen the Holy Spirit use a team the way He used yours. The excitement the youth showed when going to the parking lots to share with their friends touched my heart, but I was really moved by the numbers of kids who showed up on Saturday night for the "Jesus Cruise." Never have I seen so many young people stand up in such a bold manner to proclaim the

Good News of Jesus Christ.

Through your ministry, many lost souls were saved—souls that may have never accepted Christ if God hadn't used your ministry to burden the hearts of the youth to GO TELL.

I truly believe our county has experienced a lasting revival through your efforts. I also believe with all my heart that because of your willingness to serve, the lives of many teenagers have been permanently changed for the glory of Jesus Christ.

I pray God's richest blessings upon you and your crusade ministry.

I began to see that the most effective way to reach the maximum number of young people for Christ was through a public school assembly program. With this new strategy called ON TRACK, I began speaking in schools on the subjects of premarital sex, suicide, alcohol, drugs, and other issues concerning today's youth.

Our strategy with assembly programs was to try to reach every student in the city where we were having a crusade. Because of my football background as a player and a coach, we secured key endorsements for our nationally acclaimed assembly program. Well-known, respected coaches and athletes who believed in what we were doing participated, including football heroes like Tom Landry, Bobby Bowden, Mike Ditka, Sam Rutigliano, Grant Teaff, Steve Sloan, Dal Shealy, Terry Bradshaw, Steve Bartkowski, and others. Through these ON TRACK assemblies, we have touched more than 2 million students in our nation's schools, and thousands have come to know Christ as a result of this ministry.

Two specific stories come to mind from our ON TRACK assembly programs. One spring I was invited to speak at West High School in Wilkesboro, North Carolina. After speaking to the entire student body, the head football coach took me outside on the steps of the gymnasium.

"Do you see that hill on the other side of the football stadium?" he asked. "One of our star football players, the most sought-after offensive lineman in North Carolina, was killed on top of that hill two weeks ago while under the influence of alcohol. Late at night, driving on the wrong side of the road, he came over that hill and had a head-on collision. His football jersey is now in our trophy case as a memorial. Next to it is the jersey he would have worn at the University of North Carolina where he had just signed a full football scholarship."

As this heartbroken coach told me the story, I felt terribly sad. I wish I had been able to reach that young man before he made the decision that cost him his life.

In St. Louis, Missouri, I spoke at Hazelwood High School, one of the state's largest high schools. Following the assembly program, a seventeen-year-old girl came up to me and asked if we could talk privately. She began to tell me her sad but true story. Of all the teenagers I have counseled across this country, I don't believe I've seen one who had endured so much pain while growing up.

"When I was two years old," she said, "the courts took me away from my alcoholic mother because she was physically abusing me. When I was twelve, I ran away from home. At thirteen, I became addicted to heroin, shooting dope into my veins." With tears filling her eyes, she continued, "I'm seventeen years old. My life is a wreck. I'm labeled as a teenage alcoholic. Can you help me?"

We talked for a long time. When we got up to leave, two thoughts struck me: Does she really have a future? Does anyone really care about her? Yes, I know Someone who really cares about her because that same Person cares for me as well.

God has wonderfully and dramatically blessed my life and ministry. In 1988, Real Evangelism moved its headquarters from the Dallas/Ft. Worth area to Atlanta, Georgia. With no wife or family, I moved with the rest of the team to Atlanta.

One day, after returning on a Delta flight from Cincinnati to Atlanta, I met a young lady at the airport baggage claim who became a significant influence on me. For five years, I had been asking God to bring a mate into my life. Nine months after our first date in 1988, Lynne Peek—with her sincere, beautiful heart—became my wife. Since then, the Lord has blessed us with two beautiful daughters: Sara and Anna.

During this time, I felt a growing need to broaden my ministry beyond youth to crusade evangelism. In 1990, I launched the GO TELL Crusades Inc. Each year I speak to thousands of people in America and foreign countries through our many evangelistic events. Why? My list of reasons is long but rewarding. I want people to know the reality of their choices. I want people to know that decisions have consequences. I want people—whoever they are, whatever their ages—to be winners in this game of life. I want people to stand for Christ and against the pressures that lead to broken dreams and shattered lives.

I have lived on both sides of the fence. I thank God He gave me the chance to stand and build my life on His side before it was too late.

CHAPTER 9

COACHING A MUCH BIGGER TEAM

I'm no longer a college football coach, but I'm still coaching. Only now, instead of football strategy, drills, and plays, I'm coaching teams of people in communities throughout the country to reach their world for Jesus Christ. Just like football, we have a strategy; we have training; and we encourage each other to be the best we can be. But in this game, the stakes are eternal.

In the past several years, God has allowed me to see Him work in phenomenal ways in the lives of individuals, families, and whole communities. I want to share some amazing stories with you that remind me of the goodness and greatness of God.

Over the years, people have asked me how the culture has changed since I've been involved in communicating the Gospel. Some of those who asked this question have read reports by respected pollsters, and they have concluded that today's "postmodern" society isn't very interested in the claims of Christ. Or if people are interested, these commentators believe we have to change the way we communicate to this generation so people today can understand us. I've read these reports and heard the reasons; but I have to say that, in my experience, people are just as open and receptive to the simple and profound message of the Gospel today as they were years ago. Not long ago, in a four-day crusade in Swainsboro, Georgia, God used us to help more than 800 people make commitments to Christ. As I think about the early days of my evangelistic ministry, I remember that in a similar community, Lumberton, North Carolina, God used us to help over 700 people make commitments to Christ during a four-day event. Same message; same response.

For some reason, many who study our culture assume it's more difficult to reach people today than in years past. Of course, many advances have been made in the fields of medicine, technology, communications, and every other aspect of our society. But one thing hasn't changed in the time I've been in ministry—or in the past several thousand years: the desperate need of human hearts to know God and experience His forgiveness.

Some Christian leaders believe we have to soften our message to make it more culturally relevant for students who are growing up in unprecedented affluence. But young men and women today are hungry for purpose. They enjoy all their "toys"; but at the end of the day, they realize that all the affluence in the world can't fill the hole in their hearts. Each summer more than 5,000 students attend our GO TELL Camps. During these weeks, we communicate the incredible love of God. But as Paul said to the Corinthians, "the love of Christ compels us" to live unreservedly and unashamedly for the One who paid the price, rescued us from destruction, and entrusted to us the most challenging task the world has ever known: to take the Gospel to the entire world. Yes, we talk about God's love. In fact, we talk about it a lot; but the love of Christ not only comforts us—it compels us to take action.

Are there people today who turn up their noses at the Gospel? Certainly. Are some people so "politically correct" that they are offended when we say Jesus Christ is the only hope of mankind? Yes, of course; but that's not unique to today's culture. It was true when I started my ministry; it was true a hundred years ago, a thousand years ago, and when Jesus Himself walked the earth as the Lamb of God. There will always be people who oppose the message of the Gospel, and there will be timid Christians who are afraid of offending anyone with its powerful message. Yes, we need to be gracious and kind as we share it with those who disagree; but we never need to apologize for the message that has been entrusted to us to take to every corner of the globe.

A friend once asked me, "Rick, with all the pressures of running a nonprofit ministry of evangelistic crusades and summer camps for

During my senior year at Cameron University in Lawton, Oklahoma, we finished eighth in the nation in the final NAIA Polls (1980).

(Top row, far right)
I was the assistant football coach at Texas Tech University in Lubbock, Texas (1982).

Atlanta Falcons' All Pro Quarterback Steve Bartkowski gave his testimony at my dad's crusade in Mobile, Alabama (1984).

I was a coach at Liberty University (1985).

High school students were captivated by ON TRACK assembly in Wilkesboro, North Carolina (1988). ON TRACK has been presented to 2 million teenagers in our nation's schools, warning them of the dangers of alcohol and drug abuse.

Pastor Jay Gross leading a young man to Christ during our Montgomery County GO TELL Crusade in Conroe, Texas (2011).

With NFL Hall of Fame member Mike Ditka (1990).

Invitation response on the closing night of our Tri-County GO TELL Crusade in Anderson County, South Carolina. We saw more than 1,300 decisions for Christ (2012).

The Dallas Cowboys' legendary Tom Landry forever made his place in NFL history, but I also knew him as a great Christian. Dallas, Texas (1991).

Street evangelism with GO TELL Interns in Costa Rica (2011).

With Dr. Adrian Rogers, pastor of the historic Bellevue Baptist Church in Memphis, Tennessee (1991).

GO TELL campers having fun tubing on Lake Louise during GO TELL Camp in Toccoa, Georgia (2011).

Preaching the Gospel to young people at a school in the Dominican Republic (2009).

Meeting world-renown evangelist Dr. Billy Graham in Philadelphia (1992).

Ministering to children in a Russian orphanage, which is an annual event.

Speaking to hundreds of young people at the 5th Quarter event at Bulldog Stadium in Plainview, Texas (2011).

Baptizing a Russian orphan in the lake at GO TELL Camp in Toccoa, Georgia (1997).

With Joe Gibbs, NFL Hall of Famer, winner of three Super Bowls with the Washington Redskins, at the Daytona 500 (1998).

Distributing a Bible to a Russian man in Bryansk, Russia, during a GO TELL mission trip (1999).

Praying with a group of Russian orphans at an orphanage in Bryansk, Russia (1999).

A guest of James and Betty Robison on their *Life Today* national television program (1999).

Dallas Cowboys' All Pro Defensive Back Bill Bates gave his testimony at our Northeast Texas Crusade in Mt. Pleasant, Texas (2000).

With Dr. Jerry Falwell, Founder of Liberty University, at the Superdome in New Orleans for the Southern Baptist Convention (2001).

My brother Daniel and I with Andy Pettitte, 5-Time World Series Champion and 3-Time All-Star. The New York Yankees starting pitcher gave his testimony at our Montgomery County GO TELL Crusade in Conroe, Texas (2011).

Preaching on opening night at the Southern Baptist Convention Pastors' Conference in New Orleans, Louisiana (2001).

My good friend Bo Pilgrim, Chairman of Pilgrim Enterprises, gave his testimony at our crusade in Wheeler, Texas (2001).

My pastor James Merritt and I enjoyed the Georgia vs. Clemson football game in Athens, Georgia (2002).

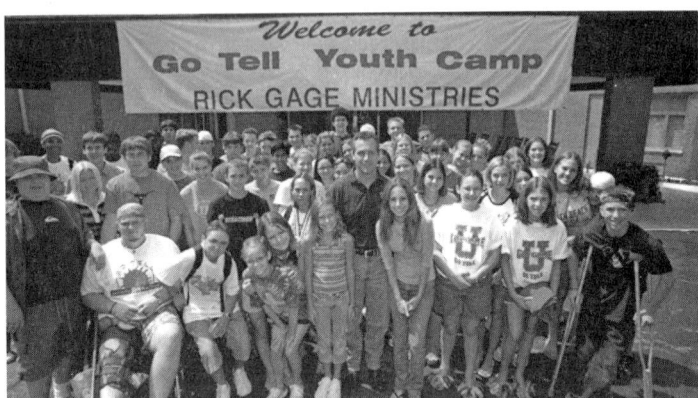

In June of 2002, this youth group from Metro Church in Garland, Texas, was involved in a tragic bus accident that made national news. A month after the accident, we flew the entire group to Atlanta to attend our GO TELL Camp in Toccoa, Georgia.

Praying for a young man who responded to a GO TELL Camp invitation after I had just preached (2002).

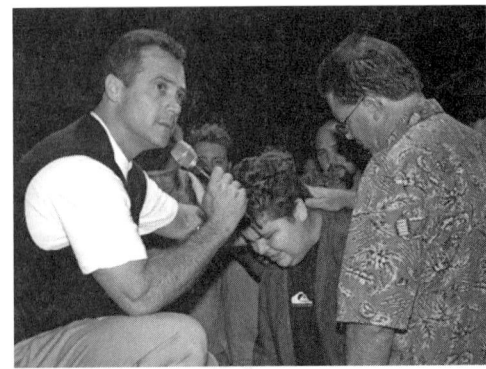

Lynne and I with University of Georgia Head Football Coach Mark Richt after he spoke at our GO TELL Camp in Toccoa, Georgia (2002).

Young and old alike make commitments to Christ at our Gainesville, Georgia Crusade (2003).

GO TELL Summer Interns in Toccoa, Georgia (2012).

Many respond to the invitation at our crusade in London, Kentucky (2003).

My beautiful wife Lynne and our precious daughters Sara and Anna (2012).

With Danny Wuerffel, former Heisman Trophy Winner from the University of Florida, 1996 National Champions, after he gave his testimony at GO TELL Camp (2005).

Closing night of our GO TELL Crusade in Dublin, Georgia (2006).

Head Football Coach Chan Gailey who has spoken at several GO TELL Camps (2005).

At our East Georgia GO TELL Crusade in Swainsboro, Georgia, we recorded 878 decisions for Christ (2005).

thousands of students, what keeps you going?" Actually, that question has an easy answer: I get up each morning with the strong, fresh sense that Almighty God has called me, the chief of sinners and the least of the saints, to serve Him. That is an awesome privilege and the biggest challenge I can possibly imagine. God has given me some abilities to reach people with the Gospel; and in fact, my purpose in life is simply an extension of Christ's life and ministry on earth two thousand years ago. I'm just following in His steps to accomplish His mission in His way for His glory.

It's such a thrill for me to see God change lives! I want to see God do in others' lives what He did in mine on that night in January of 1984 when I surrendered my life to Christ. When the Spirit of God invaded my heart on that Sunday night in Lubbock, Texas, He transformed my entire life. It was like Paul's Damascus Road experience. From the first moment of my salvation, I had a tremendous longing to know the One who died on the cross for me. I wanted to know the One who inspired the Bible. In fact, I fell in love with the Author who told me about His infinite grace and mercy toward me!

The excitement about being God's child has never left me; but like everybody else, I still get discouraged from time to time. When I talk to Christian leaders who have lost their passion for Christ and their faith that God can and will change lives, I get very disappointed. I wonder why in the world the church isn't having a far greater impact to meet the obvious needs in people's lives. In every town and city across the country, families are breaking apart; people feel alone and desperate; young people believe they have no one to trust; and old people have given up on life. These people are exactly the "lost sheep" Jesus came to save! But too many church leaders throw up their hands, focus on their problems, and passively watch as incredible opportunities for God to change lives pass them by. That discourages me very much. On the other hand, I am genuinely thrilled when I find men and women who take God at His Word, trust Him to work through them, and step out to passionately fulfill the Great Commission.

Let me share a few stories that always encourage me when I think of them. Jeremy

Ellis was a teenager on the road to nowhere. When he was only thirteen, he became addicted to alcohol and drugs. Soon he got involved in a group that would accept him: a gang. During his high school years, Jeremy wasn't interested in God. A Christian friend, though, invited him to come to a GO TELL Camp. Jeremy was interested in only two things: basketball and girls. His friend finally convinced him that our camp would have plenty of both; so Jeremy got on the bus with his friend to go to our camp in Toccoa, Georgia.

On the opening night of the camp, the prayers of Jeremy's friend were answered when Jeremy responded to the invitation and went forward. When Jeremy got to the front, the counselor asked him if he wanted to be saved. To the counselor's surprise, Jeremy said an emphatic: "No!" The counselor didn't know what to do, so he asked me to come talk to Jeremy. For the next thirty minutes, this troubled and confused young man listened as I explained the Gospel to him. During this conversation, the lights came on and Jeremy trusted Christ as his Lord and Savior. He soaked up the teaching and encouragement the rest of that week; and when he returned home, he told his whole family about God's grace in his life. Several of them responded and trusted Christ.

The transformation in this young man's life was dramatic and attractive. His bitterness melted away in the warmth of God's love. His wandering heart now found fresh purpose and direction. Instead of using people to meet his selfish desires, he now wanted God to use him to help people. Manipulation was replaced with compassion. He told me that in those first weeks, he lost half of his vocabulary because God convicted him of his foul language. Jeremy replaced curses with blessings, and God built a new man of integrity and love. Today Jeremy has been called by God to preach the Word of God. We had him speak at one of our camps not long ago, and God anointed him to touch hearts and change lives. When I think of Jeremy, I remember that with God nothing is impossible.

Recently in one of our crusades, an older lady saw a miracle she'd been praying for. She had attended church alone, week after week, for many years. Many times she had invited her husband

and grown children to go to church with her, but they simply weren't interested. When our GO TELL Crusade came to her community, God prompted her to try again; and for some reason, they came. By the last night, her husband, three children, and future son-in-law had committed their lives to Christ and were to be baptized in one of the sponsoring churches. An article about this dear lady read: "Words Cannot Describe Her Joy!" But the angels in heaven, who rejoice when a sinner repents, know exactly how she feels!

Sometimes it only takes one faithful, available person to change a family. A few years ago, a sixteen-year-old student trusted Christ at one of our summer camps. When he went home, he shared the Gospel with his parents and his sister. His father wasn't interested, but his mother and sister accepted Christ. A couple of months later, I was asked to preach one Sunday morning at that young man's home church. That morning when I gave the invitation, his father walked the aisle and came forward to receive Christ as his Lord and Savior. Now the family was complete in Christ! Years later, the pastor of that church told me that this father grew in his faith and became an outstanding lay leader in the church. The ripple effect of one high school student sharing his heart with his family continues to spread the love of God through that church and that community.

A man drove to San Saba, Texas to visit his son who was in a prison near that town. As he drove to town that night, he noticed the lights on at the football stadium. It wasn't a Friday night in the fall, so he knew it couldn't be a high school football game. He walked in and sat down at our crusade. That night God touched his lonely heart, and he committed his life to Christ. During that week, we went to the prison to share the hope of the Gospel to the prisoners. As we shared, this man's son also trusted Christ as his Savior. The two men began the week lost and hopeless, but they ended the week with more joy than they'd ever known.

The story took a tragic turn only two weeks later when the father was on his way to church on Sunday morning back home in south Texas. He was involved in a terrible car wreck, and he died from his injuries. The San Saba Crusade chairman called me to tell me about this event; and he concluded, "Rick, this man was two weeks away from hell when he came to the crusade." That's exactly right. We never know how close we are to eternity, and we never know if the message we are sharing is the last chance the listener will ever have to respond to Christ.

Sometimes people ask me: "Rick, who is your audience? Who do you try to reach with the Gospel?" I quickly answer: "Anybody who will listen." We share Christ with those who are down and out—like the man found wandering in a cemetery who hadn't been to church since the Korean War—and the up and comers—like business executives and government officials. We want to reach weak, little old ladies and strong athletes; African-American, Caucasian, Hispanic, Asian, and every other ethnic group; rich and poor; in the largest cities and the most rural areas; in our neighborhood in the suburbs of Atlanta and around the world. Jesus came to seek and to save the lost. He didn't care what people looked like or how much money they had in the bank. He only cared about what was in their hearts. That's our perspective, too.

In our office, we make calls to try to uncover some of the stories about people who have come to Christ through our ministries at camps and crusades. A phone call may tell us about an individual whose life was transformed, or a pastor may tell me a wonderful story about the changes he's seen in the life of someone who came to Christ through our ministry. But there are thousands and thousands of people we never hear about—at least not now. Someday when we are together in heaven with all of eternity to listen to one another, we'll hear, as Paul Harvey says, "the rest of the story" about many thousands of lives that God has touched. With each one, there will be laughs and tears of true joy. I look forward to that day, but I'm not quite ready for it yet. God, I trust, still has a few things for me to do here.

CHAPTER 10

KNOWING & LOVING THE GREATEST COACH OF ALL

Now I want you to meet The Coach. He is the One who showed me that becoming a Christian is a whole new game—a serious, life-changing contest that provides a full, abundant, and eternal life.

Who would you say is the greatest football coach who ever lived? Some would say Vince Lombardi or Tom Landry. Others might suggest Bill Bellicheck, Joe Gibbs, Don Shula, "Bear" Bryant, Bobby Bowden, Joe Paterno, or Bill Walsh. There are many outstanding coaches who have made unique and lasting marks upon the history of the game, and the Football Hall of Fame includes coaching giants like these.

But let me introduce you to the greatest Coach of all. He has never lost a game. In fact, He has defeated every opponent. This Coach towers above all other coaches. He is the most famous Coach who has ever lived. He has no rivals. His playbook is the most popular book of all time. The greatest Coach of all time and for all eternity is the Lord Jesus Christ.

Who is this Coach anyway? You may recall that the baby Jesus was born to a virgin named Mary. Though He was raised by Mary and her husband Joseph, His Heavenly Father is God. He was born without sin and lived obediently and righteously for all of His thirty-three years on earth.

Jesus came from the glory of heaven to the humble surroundings of a stable in Bethlehem. He grew up in a Galilean town called Nazareth, a dusty, little village without a distinguished reputation. In His lifetime, many people wondered if any good thing could come from this city. God's answer was a decisive and divine "yes."

While He was on earth, Jesus suffered rejection, temptation, ridicule, betrayal, denial, abuse, misunderstanding, mockery, and torture—and He was finally crucified, taking upon Himself the sins of the world and paying for them by His death. He died not only for the players of His own team, but He sacrificed His life even for His opponents!

Can you imagine this kind of love? What coach do you know who would give his life for his team's opponents who not only wanted to win but who also wanted to kill the coach? Jesus' opponents and even His own players were responsible for His execution. His enemies hated Him, and His friends ran away or denied they even knew Him. Their sins were the reason He went to the cross, but He forgave them. They cursed Him, but He blessed them. They spit out hate, but He poured out His love for them. That's amazing grace!

After Jesus died on the cross, brave men and women took His body and buried Him in a borrowed tomb. For them, it seemed as if the most exciting game of life had come to a tragic and senseless end. On that dark day, the glorious expectations of Jesus' disciples were shattered. Their Coach had died. The game seemed to be over.

But they had misread His playbook. On the third day, Jesus came out of the grave. He is alive! He is victor, not victim. He had told His men that He would be killed and rise from the dead, and He was true to His word.

Jesus' sacrificial death has paid the debt we owed because of our sins. His payment is a ransom to set us captives free. His bodily resurrection conquered sin and death—and opened the way for our eternal life in heaven.

Jesus Christ is Lord of the universe and now sits at the right hand of the Father, praying for us. He sent us His Spirit to convict us of sin, convert us to salvation, empower us for service, and prepare us for eternity.

But that's not all. One glorious day, this great Coach is coming back to receive the members of His team—the Church. Every one belonging to Him will be raised to live in a new heaven and a new earth. For all eternity, we'll share the joys and the blessings of Jesus Christ, the greatest Coach who ever lived.

How to Get Recruited by The Coach

Thank God that Jesus Christ recruited me, and I'm a member of God's victorious team. During my high school and college years, I was running my own life and making my own rules. I had put Jesus Christ on the bench.

But I was losing the game that really mattered. I was losing my life and my very soul. My life was in bondage, and I needed to be set free. On the night I surrendered my life to Christ, God spoke to my heart and set me free from Satan's power. That night I relinquished control and asked God to forgive me. At the feet of Coach Jesus, I totally surrendered and He became my personal Lord and Savior. Jesus Christ is now the Head Coach of my life.

Throughout the many experiences of my life, Jesus pursued me, seeking to recruit me for His team. But at each opportunity for many years, I stubbornly and arrogantly turned away by rebelling against His plan and ignoring His purpose for my life. I deeply appreciate His patience that kept pursuing me and His matchless grace that keeps loving me.

Each of us has the incredible privilege of helping others experience His grace. To a man from whom He had cast out a legion of demons, Jesus said, "Go home to your family and tell them how much the Lord has done for you, and how he has had mercy on you" (Mark 5:19). He is calling every child of God to recruit others for His team. Jesus has given us the privilege of inviting others to become a part of God's family. Are we totally committed to extend His invitation?

Jesus Christ is looking for new recruits. Because of His life, death, resurrection, and intercession, people from every corner of the globe can be redeemed from the consequences of sin and the judgment of hell. Because of what Jesus has accomplished, every young person and every adult can spend eternity in heaven as members of God's team.

Being recruited by Christ is not simply a matter of changing teams; it's a matter of allowing God's Spirit to change you! A radical transformation takes place. We become new persons with new hearts and new desires. "Therefore, if anyone is in Christ, he is a new creation; the old has gone, the new has come!" (2 Corinthians 5:17).

In John 3:3, Jesus said, "...no one can see the kingdom of God unless he is born again." Jesus wasn't referring to a physical birth. Instead He was talking about a spiritual birth. All of us are born into this world spiritually dead because of sin; and sin separates each of us from God because He is holy, just, and pure. That separation is death. Therefore, to become spiritually alive in Christ, we must be born again spiritually.

To experience this new birth, several things must happen. First, we must have knowledge of our need for salvation. Paul wrote, "...all have sinned and fall short of the glory of God" (Romans 3:23). We must know that we are lost before we can be saved.

Second, we must have knowledge of the penalty of sin. In the same letter to the people in Rome, Paul explained, "For the wages of sin is death, but the gift of God is eternal life in Christ Jesus our Lord" (Romans 6:23). An individual who works all week receives wages because he has earned them. That's what he deserves. In the same way, the Bible teaches that the wages we deserve because of our sins (that is, the payment for the sinful deeds we have done) is death. The penalty due each of us is death, eternal condemnation, and separation from God.

Third, we must have knowledge of the gift of God's provision. The penalty of sin is very real and very threatening, but there's Good News: The "gift of God" referred to in Romans 6:23 is forgiveness that cancels the penalty of sin and gives us the free gift of eternal life. Paul continued to elaborate about the meaning of Christ's death for us: "But God demonstrates his own love for us in this: While we were still sinners, Christ died for us" (Romans 5:8). Jesus has accepted the penalty of our spiritual death; therefore, He is our provision.

Finally, to be saved and spend eternity in heaven, we must be willing to respond to the Good News by surrendering our lives to Jesus Christ. Paul told the Romans: "...if you confess with your mouth, 'Jesus is Lord,' and believe in your heart that God raised him from the dead, you will be saved" (Romans 10:9). Confessing our faith in Christ with our words is the outward evidence of the heart's transformation, and believing in the heart is the inward experience. Genuine salvation of the heart overflows in the testimony of thankfulness for God's wonderful grace.

Being recruited on God's team means "to trust one's life to Jesus Christ." When we are saved, we experience changed lives. We also exchange lives. Christ takes the penalty for our sins and washes us clean; and we gladly take His right standing before God as beloved, forgiven children of the King. (2 Corinthians 5:21) We now belong to Him. He now dwells in us to love and forgive others through us!

Has Jesus Christ personally recruited you? Have you ever said "yes" to Him? If you have, take a minute to reflect on God's grace toward you and thank Him. If there's any doubt that you're on His team, don't wait any longer. Respond to His gracious invitation to trust in Him and enjoy the forgiveness He offers. Pray this prayer (or use words of your own) and ask Jesus to become the Head Coach of your life:

Lord Jesus, I know that I am a sinner in need of Your forgiveness. I believe that You died for my sins. I am turning from my sin and turning to You to be my Lord and Savior. I am asking You to take control of my life right now. Amen.

There is nothing magical about these words. All it takes is a genuine, repentant heart. If you pray this prayer (or a similar one) and give Christ your heart and mind, you will receive a life that is exciting and eternal—"Christ in you" (Colossians 1:27).

The following words from Scripture will help you remember what God has promised to all who turn to Him. Paul promised, "Everyone who calls on the name of the Lord will be saved" (Romans 10:13). And John assured us that we can have tremendous confidence in God's promise to give us eternal life. He wrote: "I write these things to you who believe in the name of the Son of God so that you may know that you have eternal life" (1 John 5:13).

Throughout these many years of proclaiming the Gospel, I've seen thousands pray a prayer of repentance and invite Christ to become their Savior. In one crusade, a young man gave his life to Christ and, after returning home, led several of his family members to Him. He started a Bible Club at school which averages more than

100 young people every week. He actively serves in the youth ministry of his church and believes God is calling him to preach the Gospel.

If you still haven't said "yes" to Christ's invitation to follow Him and become a member of His team, try to identify what is keeping you from becoming a part of Christ's team today. You'll find that any resistance you feel is insignificant compared to the incredible riches of knowing and loving Christ!

Learning to Play the Game His Way

When we become a part of God's team, it's imperative that we follow His game plan for our lives. The Bible declares that the first step of obedience for a new Christian is to follow Christ in believer's baptism. Jesus commanded us to go and make disciples and baptize them. (Matthew 28:19)

What is baptism? It's a powerful, visible symbol. Going into and out of the water identifies us with Jesus Christ's death, burial, and resurrection. Baptism also proclaims our faith in Him to our family, friends, and community.

It's a way of saying, "I belong to Jesus Christ."

Baptism is an outward expression of an inward reality. It doesn't indicate that believers are completely mature, but it says we are obedient in what God commands us to do.

Once we have obeyed the command of baptism, we are now ready to continue the game of life—God's way. An athlete exercises to be the strongest, fastest, and best athlete he or she can become. Christians must apply this same kind of discipline in becoming the best Christians we can be for the Lord by allowing Christ to express Himself through our personalities. We simply can't produce godly attitudes and actions on our own. Jesus told His disciples: "... apart from me you can do nothing" (John 15:5). But trusting in God's strength and guided by Him, we can accomplish amazing things for His glory. Paul encouraged the people of Philippi: "I can do everything through him who gives me strength" (Philippians 4:13).

In His Great Commission, Jesus said that as His disciples spread the Good News, they should teach new believers to obey everything He commanded them. (Matthew 28:20) Every disciple of Christ, each member of His team must learn to obey the truths and follow the plan Jesus teaches in His Word.

When a football player reports to training camp, he is given a playbook to study, learn, and live by. The Bible is God's playbook. We need to study it carefully and regularly to learn God's principles and doctrine. The Apostle Paul instructed Timothy: "Do your best to present yourself to God as one approved, a workman who does not need to be ashamed and who correctly handles the word of truth" (2 Timothy 2:15). To respond appropriately to temptation and experience God's power and purpose every day, we need to understand the doctrine of sin, the doctrines of Christ and the Holy Spirit, and the doctrine of the church. We must put into practice the doctrine of living a victorious Christian life and the doctrine of preparing for Christ's return.

We also need to meditate upon God's Word each day. Joshua told the people of Israel, "Do not let this Book of the Law depart from your mouth; meditate on it day and night, so that you may be careful to do everything written in it. Then you will be prosperous and successful" (Joshua 1:8).

I find it helpful to memorize a portion of God's Word every week. I also try to apply specific Scriptures to my thoughts, relationships, attitudes, and actions.

As Christians, we also must spend time in prayer daily. The famous English preacher Charles Spurgeon said, "True prayer is an approach of the soul by the Spirit of God to the throne of God."

Someone has said, "Where there is much prayer, there is much power." I know this to be true. The best place to observe and learn the truths of Christ is in an encouraging and exciting, Bible-believing church. If you're not currently attending a strong, Christ-centered church, find a pastor who preaches and teaches God's Word and people who experience God's Word in a community of faith.

A church home provides a network of Christian friends and support to encourage you, guide you, and pray for you. I'm thankful for this kind of network of wonderful friends and supporters in my home church, Cross Pointe

Church, where James Merritt is the pastor.

In addition, a solid church foundation will provide opportunities for us to help others in their Christian walk. Involvement in a local church gives us proper training for evangelism and discipleship, so we can introduce others to The Coach and help them grow strong in loving and serving Him.

Introducing Others to The Coach

The greatest thing a person can do is to bring another person to Christ. In fact, introducing others to Jesus Christ is the greatest work that God allows us to do while we live on this earth.

Immediately after I was saved, I began sharing what Christ had done in my heart. The Lord had radically changed every part of my being, and I was in no way ashamed of what He had done in my life. I wanted others to receive what Christ had given me. How could I withhold a precious, life-changing gift that had set me free and transformed my life forever?

Jesus commands every Christian to be a witness for Him. Before He ascended to the

Father, Jesus told His followers: "... you will receive power when the Holy Spirit comes on you; and you will be my witnesses in Jerusalem [your city], and in all Judea [your county] and Samaria [your state], and to the ends of the earth" (Acts 1:8). The heartbeat of a church should be to win people to Christ. The mark of a great church is the living reality of men and women, young and old with a vision and compassion to reach lost people.

John Wesley, the great English theologian and evangelist, reminds us: "We have only one job on earth: save souls." The Apostle Paul communicated his intense passion for others to know Christ: "I speak the truth in Christ—I am not lying, my conscience confirms it in the Holy Spirit—I have great sorrow and unceasing anguish in my heart. For I could wish that I myself were cursed and cut off from Christ for the sake of my brothers, those of my own race.... my heart's desire and prayer to God...is that they may be saved" (Romans 9:1-3, 10:1).

Every believer whose heart is in tune with Christ has a desire to lead others to Christ. As soon as I was saved, I asked God to use me to touch people's lives with His Gospel. Through His grace and power, I've had the privilege to personally introduce thousands of people to Him. One particular occasion stands out. On a Delta flight from Atlanta to Dallas, I began to witness to the lady sitting next to me. During that two-hour flight, she listened to my entire testimony. When we arrived in Dallas, she said she wasn't ready to give her life to Christ but she appreciated my sharing with her what God had done in my life.

A few weeks later, I received this letter from that lady. She wrote:

Dear Rick,

I wanted to say how much I enjoyed visiting with you on the plane from Atlanta to Dallas. My thoughts and prayers are with you in your sharing of God's Word. I now know how you are rejoicing since you gave your life to Jesus Christ.

One night just three weeks ago, I was saved. When I came so close to entering Satan's world, I asked Jesus to come into my life. Praise God! God bless you, Rick. I know He put you in my life for a reason.

This letter dramatically proves a simple but powerful fact: We never know the impact we can have on someone's life when we are obedient to what God has commanded us to do.

In Laurel, Mississippi, a seventeen-year-old man surrendered to the ministry and served as one of our crusade counselors. That week he led his mom, dad, grandfather, and several other relatives and friends to Christ. Today Steve Nixon is an ordained Southern Baptist pastor in Laurel, Mississippi; and he is being mightily used of God.

In Stockbridge, Georgia, I spoke to several thousand students in the schools of Henry County. After one of our ON TRACK assemblies, a young teenage girl shared with me her problems and the troubles she was facing. She showed me the scars on her wrist where she had attempted suicide by using a razor blade. Hearing her tragic story, I began to share with her how much Christ loved and cared for her. I had the privilege of leading her to Jesus. I invited her to come hear me preach that night at Mount Vernon Baptist Church. She came forward during the invitation time to make her decision public. The next night she returned and was baptized. The following night she brought a friend, and her friend was saved. Today this delightful, young lady is actively involved at Mount Vernon Baptist Church in Stockbridge, Georgia.

One Sunday morning in Kissimmee, Florida, I was driving to preach at a scheduled revival service. On the way, I picked up two hitchhikers and took them to church with me. That morning in the pastor's office, I shared the Gospel story and led both of them to Christ. After the service, I took them out to eat and put them up in a room for the rest of the afternoon. That night they returned to the church and were both baptized. Who knows how many hitchhikers have heard their testimony of Christ?

A similar experience took place in Wilkesboro, North Carolina. We took all the young people out witnessing prior to the evening services. A group of us had stopped at a convenience store and saw a young couple on a motorcycle. We began to witness to them and encouraged them to attend our crusade service that night. They told us they weren't from Wilkesboro. They were simply passing through town, but their motorbike had broken down and needed a battery. We told them: "If you attend the crusade service, we'll help you get your motorcycle fixed and buy you a new battery."

They agreed to attend the service. It was the first time they had ever attended a Gospel service. That night we fed them and paid for their lodging, and the next day we arranged to get their motorcycle fixed. Instead of leaving town, they chose to stay and attend the crusade the rest of the week. On Monday night, both of them gave their hearts to Christ. Perhaps there are motorcycle riders across America who have met Christ as a result of the witness of these two who stayed because we showed them some kindness and shared the message of Christ with them.

David Wellborn was a young man whose father was a pastor. David had been living in sinful rebellion for many years while professing to be a Christian. During a citywide crusade in Boone, North Carolina, David surrendered his life to Christ. Today David is a pastor, leading a congregation to know and share Christ. He is preaching, teaching, and witnessing; and he is introducing others to Jesus Christ.

You, too, can become a powerful witness and lead others to Christ. Wherever you are, whatever your circumstances, you can go—you can go tell—you can go tell others about Jesus. Charles Spurgeon once said: "He who converts a soul draws water from a fountain, but he who trains a soul winner digs a well from which thousands may drink to eternal life."

Thousands are waiting to drink from your well. Will you join Coach Jesus in life's greatest adventure?

"Where there is no vision, the people perish..." (Proverbs 29:18, KJV). Ask God to give you a vision—a vision to tell the world about Jesus Christ, The Greatest Coach of all time!

About Rick Gage

 In 1986, Rick Gage walked away from a promising career coaching football and surrendered his life to full-time evangelistic ministry. A few years later, he became the founder of GO TELL Crusades, Inc. He has been conducting evangelistic events around the world and has seen tens of thousands make commitments to the Lord Jesus Christ.

Roger Alford of the Associated Press wrote, "Gage fills stadiums just as full as the Rev. Billy Graham does. It's just that the stadiums are much smaller. The Texas native takes his GO TELL Crusades to the small towns that other preachers might see only from the air on their way to big cities. Like Graham, Gage preaches the same Gospel, offers the same invitation to would-be believers, and sees multitudes walk toward the platform to accept Christ."

Rick is also the founder of GO TELL Ministries. His annual GO TELL Youth Camps, which began in 1989, have reached tens of thousands of students and their leaders from churches across the country. These summer camps have helped thousands of students come to Christ or surrender to full-time ministry.

To further impact the youth of America, Rick has delivered his nationally acclaimed "ON TRACK" assembly program to more than 2 million teenagers in our nation's schools. This program confronts young people's abuse of drugs and alcohol. In addition, he has appeared on numerous radio and television programs. He is the author of his autobiography, *More Than a Game*, and a Bible study, *Download*, which helps young people and adults grow in their faith.

For fun, Rick enjoys jogging, working out, and hunting. Rick, his wife Lynne, and their daughters Sara and Anna live near Atlanta, Georgia.

About GO TELL Ministries

Educators, coaches, pastors, city officials, sports personalities, and politicians nationwide have acclaimed Rick Gage's profound impact on young people. He is considered an authority on youth culture and the pressures faced by today's students.

Rick has spoken face-to-face to more than 2 million students in America's public schools through his nationally acclaimed ON TRACK  assembly program. This hard-hitting, honest talk on the realities of life among today's youth has transformed the attitudes and destinies of hundreds of thousands of young people in the United States.

As one of today's most sought-after youth communicators, Rick is also an internationally known evangelist. He has led thousands of people—young and old, rich and poor of all ethnic backgrounds—to make personal decisions to live for Christ.

God has given Rick a tremendous vision to

fulfill the Great Commission. As a result of this vision, GO TELL Crusades, Inc. was founded in 1990 with its headquarters in the Atlanta area. Other outreaches of this evangelistic ministry include:

GO TELL Crusades in football stadiums, drawing tens of thousands from cities and surrounding regions for a major evangelistic event.

GO TELL Youth Camps, attracting tens of thousands of students and youth leaders from churches nationwide to be equipped in evangelism and discipleship.

GO TELL Summer Internships to train the next generation of Godly leaders as camp ministry interns and short-term missionaries.

GO TELL Missions to share God's love with those who have never heard the Gospel and to help meet their physical needs.

GO TELL Crusades, Inc. and GO TELL Ministries, Inc. constantly have new opportunities to present the Good News of

Jesus Christ, and we praise Him for the many lives we continue to see changed by His power. With the Apostle Paul, we say, "...pray for us that the message of the Lord may spread rapidly and be honored, just as it was with you" (2 Thessalonians 3:1).

As you've been reading this book, perhaps God has touched your heart and you'd like to help this ministry accomplish the mission God has given us. GO TELL Ministries, Inc. is a nonprofit organization. If you'd like to contribute to our ministry of reaching the lost and changing lives, send a tax-deductible donation to GO TELL Ministries. We'd really appreciate it! And if you have any questions about how you can contribute regularly, contact us by phone, mail, or email.

For more information, please visit our web site at: www.gotellministries.com

Contact Us

We Want to Hear from You!

You may have questions about your relationship with Christ, or you may just want to tell us what God has done in your life. Maybe you want to ask us to pray for you, or maybe you feel you are at the end of the road and you have no one else to turn to. Whatever the reason, please contact us. We'd love to hear from you.

Find us on the web at:
gotellministries.com
Email us at:
info@gotellministries.com
Or mail to:
GO TELL Ministries
P.O. Box 2138
Duluth, GA 30096

A Note from Rick

Welcome to the GO TELL Ministries family! I want you to know we are praying for you. I hope you will continue to pray for my family, this ministry, and me as we take the message of Christ to people all over America and around the world.

If this book has spoken to your heart or you have specific prayer needs, please contact us. We'll join you in bringing your needs before the Throne of Grace. God bless you!

"I thank my God every time I remember you. In all my prayers for all of you, I always pray with joy" (Philippians 1:3-4).

Resources

God has used *More Than a Game* to help many people come to Christ and to encourage many believers to develop more of a passion to love and serve Him. Perhaps you know

a friend or family member who could benefit from Rick's message. If you would like to get multiple copies, GO TELL Ministries offers a substantial discount for you to give books to members of Sunday school classes, Bible studies, and organizations.

To Order More Copies

Go online to www.gotellministries.com

Or write to:

GO TELL Ministries
P.O. Box 2138
Duluth, GA 30096

Also Available...

God has given you incredible resources. Learn to use them, so you can grow strong in Christ!

Thousands of people are gaining insight into their relationship with Christ from *Download*. Many are using it to study the Bible and apply life-changing truths on their own, but many more are using it for stimulating group study and discussions. For more information about this Bible study booklet, go to: gotellministries.com.

Addressing students at Liberty University during the presentation of the American Bible Society Pilgrim Award. The award was given to Chancellor Jerry Falwell, Jr.

2014

Photo Credit: Photo by David Duncan/Liberty University

Receiving the prestigious Pilgrim Award for Workplace Evangelism from the American Bible Society. (l-r: Gil Stricklin, Rick Gage, Bo Pilgrim, Lynne Gage & Simon Barnes.)

2010

With Mayor Leticia Salazar of Matamoros, Mexico and our Crusade Youth Chairman Alfredo Macias. Ms. Salazar gave a testimony on opening night of our crusade.

2014

GO TELL Summer Interns

2014

Campers at GO TELL Camp making spiritual decisions for Christ.

2013

Coach Mark Richt and his wife Katharyn with Lynne & I during our 25th Anniversary of GO TELL Camps.

2013

Preaching the Gospel on Youth Night during the ARK LA TEX GO TELL Crusade in Center, Texas.

2013

A Crusade Counselor praying with young ladies in the end zone at the Sulphur River GO TELL Crusade in Cooper, Texas.

2013

We led this Juarez, Mexico college football team to Christ during our Juarez Crusade. Through the help of GO TELL supporters, we provided the team with new equipment & uniforms. 2013

With family members & head coach of the Big Black Jaguares in Jaurez, Mexico.

This team made national news after the death of two of its players during a massacre in 2010.

2013

Invitation response during our GO TELL Crusade in Juarez, Mexico.

We saw more than 4,000 make commitments to Christ.

2013

Invitation response on the closing night at our Red River Valley GO TELL Crusade in Paris, Texas. About 1,000 decisions for Christ were made during the four-night evangelistic event.

2014

Cowboy Church pastor, Duane Hamil, leading a young lady to Jesus during our Red River Valley GO TELL Crusade in Paris, Texas.

2014

Several thousand attend the first night of the Lake Cumberland GO TELL Crusade in Pulaski County, Kentucky.

2014

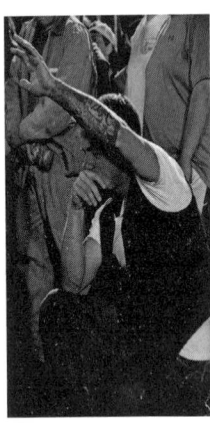

A man on his knees getting right with God at our Lake Cumberland GO TELL Crusade in Pulaski County, Kentucky.

2014

Invitation response during the Free State GO TELL Crusade in Van, Texas, where 847 decisions for Christ were made during the four-night event.

2014

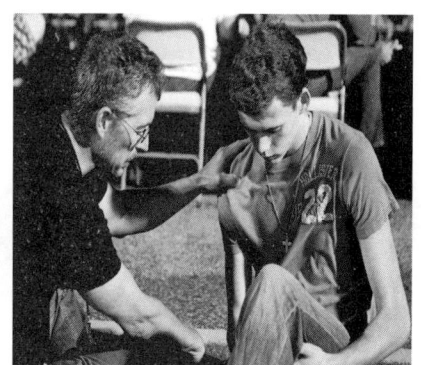

A crusade counselor praying with a young man after the invitation response at the Free State GO TELL Crusade in Van, Texas.

2014

Invitation response during the Marshall County GO TELL Crusade in Guntersville, Alabama. Over 1,300 total commitments were made to Christ during the four-night event.

2013

Invitation response on opening night of the Coal Country GO TELL Crusade in Bell County, Kentucky.

2014